Making Headway
Intermediate

Everyday Listening and Speaking

Sarah Cunningham
Peter Moor

Oxford University Press

Oxford University Press
Walton Street, Oxford OX2 6DP

Oxford New York
Athens Auckland Bangkok Bombay
Calcutta Cape Town Dar es Salaam Delhi
Florence Hong Kong Istanbul Karachi
Kuala Lumpur Madras Madrid Melbourne
Mexico City Nairobi Paris Singapore
Taipei Tokyo Toronto

and associated companies in
Berlin Ibadan

OXFORD and OXFORD ENGLISH are trade marks of
Oxford University Press

ISBN 0 19 435502 0

© Oxford University Press 1992
First published 1992
Third impression 1995

No unauthorized photocopying

Typeset by Tradespools Ltd, Frome, Somerset

Printed in Malta
by Interprint Limited

Acknowledgements
The publishers and authors would like to
thank the following for their kind permission
to reproduce copyright material:

Mr and Mrs K Peros
Cotswold Lodge Hotel
Oxford

Graphic Thought Facility for the poster for
the Royal Shakespeare Company production
of *The Last Days of Don Juan*

Stylo Rouge for the poster for the Royal Ballet
production of *Cyrano*
(Photography by Karl Grant)

Illustrations by
Anna Brookes
Nigel Paige

Location photography
Emily Andersen

Studio photography
Graham Alder

The publishers would also like to thank the
following for their participation in location
photography and/or for the use of their
premises:

The Chepstow London
Cotswold Lodge Hotel Oxford
The Dôme Oxford
Freuds Oxford
Dr Euphan Hunter
The Hyde Park Hotel London
The Lacquer Chest London
Mahogany Oxford
Joel Mishcon
Mr & Mrs Jin Nakagawa
Palio Pastafino London
The Old Parsonage Hotel Oxford
Pitcher and Piano London
Royal College of Art London
Rumbelows London
Simpsons in The Strand London

Contents

Foreword

Everyday Listening and Speaking

Language skills rarely exist in isolation. We often write in reaction to something we have read, just as we often comment on what we have heard on the radio or seen on the television. The skills of listening and speaking are probably the ones given most prominence in the modern language classroom as they are the skills of everyday interaction and, as such, they are completely interdependent. When ordering a meal, booking a hotel room, or looking for somewhere to live, it is not enough for language users to know what they themselves want to say. They must react to the situation and to the language they are confronted with, and then amend their response accordingly.

Class time provides the opportunity to rehearse how the foreign language is used in the real world. This book develops the two skills of listening and speaking in a highly systematic and practical manner. The authors have carefully selected a range of situations that visitors to an English-speaking country could well find themselves in. The better these can be practised in advance, the more successful the learners' actual performance will be.

Students' interest will be engaged by the practicality of the topics. We feel sure they will find the tasks relevant, challenging, and enjoyable. New language is presented and contextualized, and known language is developed via the extensive practice activities.

Teachers of lower levels are constantly looking out for ways of engaging their students in fluent conversation; interesting listening material based on everyday situations is also much appreciated. This book provides both. Teachers can select a topic which is appropriate to their class, and they will be able to rely on the material to provide a thorough, balanced lesson or series of lessons.

John and Liz Soars
Series editors

Introduction

Students This book is for young adults at intermediate level who want to use English to travel and would like to practise the type of language they will meet in real, everyday situations.

Teachers This book is for teachers using *Headway Intermediate* or any other intermediate course. It provides additional listening material which links in smoothly with popular themes like health, travel, or technology.

How the book is organized

Each of the fourteen units takes about one to one and a half hours of class time. The main focus of each unit is a taped conversation or conversations, and listening and speaking are practised equally.

Each unit is divided into four parts:

Before you listen This creates interest in the topic and prepares the student for key vocabulary and culture-specific expressions.

Listening for information provides tasks aimed at general comprehension or comprehension of specific information in the text. The students are not expected or encouraged to follow every word of the conversation. Often they are expected to listen to a conversation more than once and are given a different task each time they listen. This develops confidence and helps them to build up a fuller understanding of the text.

Listening for language This gives intensive listening practice by focusing on short extracts from the conversations in more detail. As well as helping to improve listening skills, these activities draw the students' attention to useful expressions and structures which they are then encouraged to practise in preparation for the **Speaking** activity.

Speaking Through roleplay activities, the students act out some of the situations they have encountered in the listenings, and may encounter in real life. They provide the opportunity to use in context language that has been isolated in the unit. The activities are structured in a variety of ways, encouraging the students to use the language creatively, while providing clear guidance and ideas to stimulate the imagination.

The tapescripts and answer key at the end of this book help the teacher and allow the students to use the book independently.

How to use the book

Most activities in the book are self-explanatory. However, here are a few general hints to help the teacher and the students.

To the teacher

1 It is important to prepare the students for the topic before a listening, so it is not advisable to omit the first section. But if time is short, the discussion questions in this section can be dealt with very briefly.

2 It is a good idea to focus the students on the first task or questions *before* playing the tape, as this gives the initial listening far greater purpose.

3 If the students find the listenings difficult, it may be necessary to replay the tape several times. In the long-term, however, it is better training for the students' listening skills if you play the texts all the way through, rather than stopping at the answer to each question.

4 If time is short, the activities in the **Listening for language** section could be omitted. However, they do pre-teach useful items for the speaking activities at the end of each unit, and provide a good opportunity for you to correct pronunciation, etc.

5 The rolecards, questions, etc. in the **Speaking** section are invaluable in preparing the students to speak, so give them enough time to prepare.

6 It is important for intermediate students' confidence to have the opportunity to express themselves freely in English, even if they make a lot of mistakes. This will be easier if you keep a low profile at the **Speaking** stage, and do not correct too much.

7 Try to do the activities in the order given, as they are intended to build up the students' confidence and understanding systematically.

To the student working independently

1 Even if you cannot discuss the questions in the **Before you listen** section with another student, read them and think about them, as this will help you to understand the conversations on the tape better.

2 Read the questions in the **Listening for information** section *before* you listen to the tape and *only* try to answer these questions. You do not need to understand every word on the tape!

3 Try to listen to the whole conversation. Don't stop the tape after every few words. In real life, you usually can't 'stop the tape'!

4 You may want to read the tapescripts at the back of the book. But try to do this *after* you have finished the listening tasks.

5 After you have done the **Listening for language** activities, you could *record* yourself and compare your pronunciation to that on the tape.

6 If you can, find a friend to do the **Speaking** activities with. If not, write or act out the conversation by yourself!

1 Getting around

Before you listen

1 All the words in the box relate to transport. Put them into the correct column below. (Some words can go in more than one column.)

*A 'two-storey' British bus

a fare	a double-decker*	passengers	a platform
to change lines	the tube	a conductor	a return ticket
a departure board	to drop someone off	a single ticket	

Train	Underground	Aeroplane	Bus	Taxi
a fare				

2 Work in pairs. Discuss the following questions.
- Which forms of transport do you prefer for long journeys?
- What about when you travel around in your own town or city?
- Do you use public transport very much? What is it like in your local area? Could it be better, do you think?
- Have you ever tried to use public transport in a foreign city? Was it easy or difficult?

Listening for information

Ray lives in New York. He is coming to Europe on holiday. He wants to visit his friend, David, in England.

David lives in Brighton, on the south coast of England. He met Ray on holiday in New York last year.

T.1a

1   Listen to the first part of Ray and David's conversation and answer the questions below.

a. Why is Ray coming to Europe?

_____

b. When is he arriving in England?

_____

c. Why can't David come to London to meet him?

_____

d. What is David going to tell Ray next?

_____

T.1b   ⌐○

2   Listen to the second part of their conversation. Which of these forms of transport will Ray use, and in what order?

a. ☐

b. ☐

c. **1**

d. ☐
⌐○

e. ☐

f. ☐

T.1b

3 Look at the notes that Ray made during the conversation. Listen again to the second part, and fill in the gaps.

From Heathrow, Underground →
_____ station (Piccadilly Line –
takes about ___ minutes).

Bus number ___ or ___ to Victoria (bus
stop _____ tube station).**

From Victoria, fast train to Brighton at
___ minutes past the hour (takes _____
_____). (Other trains take an
_____.)

David's Office
Davis International,
_____ Road.

Listening for language

T.1c

1 You will hear ten things that Ray heard or said during his journey from Heathrow to Brighton. Say if he was in a tube, a bus, a train, or a taxi at the time.

Ray heard

1 bus _____
2 _____
3 _____
4 _____
5 _____

Ray said

6 _____
7 _____
8 _____
9 _____
10 _____

2 Now look at the sentences that you heard on the tape. Can you fill in the gaps?

1 _____ more fares, please?

2 We apologize for the _____ of the 10.06 service to Brighton.

3 Stand clear of the _____, please...let the _____ off first, please.

4 _____ 15 for the 10.32 service to Brighton, _____ at Clapham Junction, East Croydon, Redhill, Gatwick Airport, Three Bridges...

5 _____ do you want me to drop you?

6 Excuse me, is this the _____ train for Brighton?

7 It's OK, you can _____ the change.

8 Excuse me, can you tell me where I can _____ a bus to Victoria, please?

9 Excuse me, is this seat _____?

10 _____ to Victoria, please.

◀ | T.1c | 🔑—0

3 Listen and check your answers.

4 Practise saying the expressions that Ray used. Copy the voice on the tape.

Speaking

1 Work in pairs. Look at the pictures below. What do you think the tourist is saying in each case? In which of the situations do you think the two people might start up a conversation? What sort of things might they talk about?

2 Act out each conversation with your partner.

2 Going out

1 How often do you go out in the evening? Which of these things do you do most often? Which is your favourite way of spending the evening?

go for a walk

visit friends

go out for a drink

go to the cinema

go out for a meal with a group of friends

go to a disco

go to the theatre

do sports

go to a concert (pop/jazz/classical)

go out alone with your partner

Which do you rarely or never do? Why not?

Which are the most popular evening entertainments in your country? Do you know anything about evening entertainments in Britain? What kinds of entertainment is London well known for?

2 You will hear two young women arranging an evening out in London. Below are some of the words they use to do this. Can you guess where they are arranging to go?

the stalls	a musical	the evening performance
the dress circle	a ticket agency	a row (of seats)

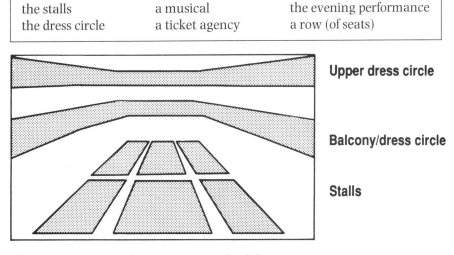

Upper dress circle

Balcony/dress circle

Stalls

Check the meaning of any words you don't know.

Listening for information

Aileen, who comes from Edinburgh, is in London for a few days for an important conference. She is having a drink with her friend, Cindy, in a wine bar.

T.2a

1 Listen to Aileen and Cindy's conversation and answer these questions.

a. When is Aileen travelling back to Edinburgh?

_____

b. What would Aileen like to do on Saturday night?

_____

c. What problem does Cindy mention?

_____

d. What does Cindy find in the newspaper?

_____

e. What do they decide to do in the end?

_____

T.2b

2 Cindy phones the agency the next day. She manages to book some tickets for Saturday night. Listen to her phone call and decide which of the tickets opposite are the ones that she buys.

a.

b.

c.

d.

e.

Listening for language

T.2c

1 In their conversation in the wine bar, Cindy and Aileen make *suggestions* and *arrangements* for their evening out. Look at the pairs of phrases below. Only *one* of each pair is used in their conversation. Listen to part of the conversation again, and underline the phrase that is used. The first one has been done for you.

1a. So, are you doing anything on Saturday night, then?
  b. So, will you be free on Saturday night, then?

2a. Well, I haven't got anything planned...
  b. Well, I'm not doing anything special...

3a. Then let's do something special, shall we?
  b. Then I think we should do something special...

4a. Yeah, fantastic idea!
  b. Yeah, that's a great idea!

5a. What do you want to do?
  b. What do you fancy doing?

6a. Why don't we get tickets for something really good?
  b. How about getting tickets for something really good?

2 Practise saying the phrases that you heard. Copy the voices on the tape.

Speaking

Work in groups. You are all in London together, and decide to have a special night out before you all go home at the end of next week. Decide:

- which night would be best for everyone (each person should decide which nights they will be free, and what they are doing on other nights).
- what you would like to see (a film, a ballet, a concert, a musical, etc.).
- which of the performances below you would all like to see.
- which one you will go to if there are no seats for your first choice.
- *who* is going to book the seats.

In your conversation, use some of the phrases on page 13.

Apollo Victoria
Starlight Express a musical by Andrew Lloyd Weber, directed by Trevor Nunn. Mon-Sat 7.45pm £8-£22.50.

Drury Lane Theatre Royal
Miss Saigon by Alain Boublil and Claude-Michel Schonberg, directed by Nicholas Hytner. Mon-Sat 7.45pm £7.75-£28.00.

Fortune Theatre
The Woman in Black a play by Susan Hill, directed by Robin Herford. Mon-Thurs £7-£17. Fri-Sat £8-£18.

Garrick Theatre
Kvetch a play written and directed by Steven Berkoff. Mon-Fri 8pm Sat 5 & 8.30 pm £5.50-£16.

Haymarket Theatre Royal
Becket by Jean Anouilh, directed by Elijah Moshinsky. Mon-Sat 7.30 pm £8.50-£20.

Her Majesty's
The Phantom of the Opera a musical by Andrew Lloyd Weber, directed by Harold Prince. Mon-Sat 7.45pm £8.75-£28 (sold out for the next six months).

London Palladium
Joseph and the Amazing Technicolor Dreamcoat a musical by Andrew Lloyd Weber, directed by Steven Pimlott. Mon-Sat 7.30 pm £8.50-£27.50.

Old Vic
Carmen Jones a musical by Oscar Hammerstein II, directed by Simon Callow. Mon-Sat 7.45pm £20.50-£30; restricted views £8.50-£20.50.

Palace Theatre
Les Misérables a musical by Alain Boublil and Claude-Michel Schonberg, directed by Trevor Nunn and John Caird. Mon-Sat 7.30 pm £5.50-£27.50.

Queen's Theatre
Waiting for Godot a play by Samuel Beckett, directed by Les Blair. Mon-Thurs 8pm; Fri & Sat 8.45 pm £8.50-£18.50.

RSC Barbican
A Woman of No Importance a play by Oscar Wilde, directed by Philip Prowse. Fri-Sat 7.30 pm £6.50-£19.

Richard II by Shakespeare, directed by Ron Daniels. Wed 7.30pm. £6.50-£19.

RSC The Pit
The Last Days of Don Juan by Tirso de Molina, directed by Danny Boyle. Mon-Thurs 7.30pm. £10.50-£12.50.

Wyndham's Theatre
The Ride Down Mount Morgan a play by Arthur Miller, directed by Michael Blakemore. Mon-Sat 7.30pm £9-£20.

3 Dealing with money

1 What currency is used in your country? What coins/notes are there?

2 Here are some British coins and banknotes. Find out what the *exchange rate* is for your currency.

How much is each coin or note worth in your currency?

3 Look at the three pictures below. Each person has a problem connected with money. What do you think it is?

4 Which of these three people

– wants to *cash a cheque?*
– has *the wrong change?*
– needs *some change?*

– will have to pay *commission?*
– will be given a *receipt?*

Listening for information

T.3a

You will hear three dialogues about the situations in the pictures in 3 above.

1 Tim and Claire are waiting for their friends, Liz and Chris, in a pub. Liz and Chris are late, so Tim decides to telephone them. Listen to the dialogue and tick (√) the correct answer.

a. Liz and Chris's phone number is

☐ 63800 ☐ 63008 ☐ 63088

b. What money does Tim have?

☐ ☐ ☐

c. How does Tim get his change?

☐ from Claire ☐ from the barman ☐ he finds some in his pocket

d. What change does he get?

☐  ☐  ☐

Check your answers.

T.3b

2 Mr Graham is an American tourist who wants to cash a traveller's cheque in a bank. Fill in the details on his receipt.

LAMBERT'S BANK PLC	Currency Exchange Receipt
Cash/Traveller's cheque	*Traveller's Cheque*
Currency	
Exchange Rate	
Amount	
Gross Total	*£57.17*
Commission	
Net Total	

Check your answers.

T.3c

3 a. Listen to the dialogue. What does Suzie buy in the newsagent's? Tick the correct picture.

2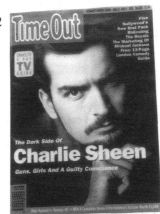

3

b. How much do the things cost? _____

c. How much does she give the newsagent? _____

d. How much change does she get? _____

e. What's the problem? _____

17

Listening for language

1 Here are some extracts from the three dialogues. In each, the second half of the first sentence is missing. Try to work out what the missing words are.

1 Have you got _____?

I'll have a look... um... No, sorry.

4 What's the _____?

It's...57.17 pence to the dollar.

2 Can you change _____?

Sure. What would you like? A fifty and five tens?

5 Sorry, I think you've _____ _____.

Oh? What's that?

3 Can you tell me where _____ _____?

Yes. If you just go to the 'Foreign' counter...

6 I think you've given me _____ _____.

Are you sure?

T.3d Listen and check your answers.

2 Practise saying the phrases with a partner. Copy the voices on the tape.

Speaking

1 Here are the opening lines of three dialogues. Where do you think the speakers are in each dialogue?

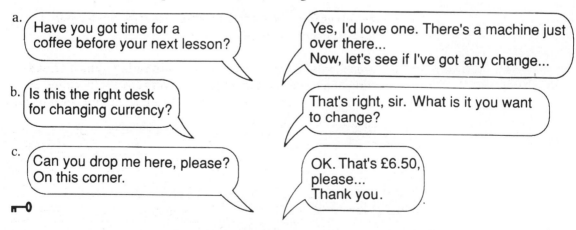

a. Have you got time for a coffee before your next lesson?

Yes, I'd love one. There's a machine just over there...
Now, let's see if I've got any change...

b. Is this the right desk for changing currency?

That's right, sir. What is it you want to change?

c. Can you drop me here, please? On this corner.

OK. That's £6.50, please...
Thank you.

2 With a partner, continue *two* of the dialogues. Introduce a small problem or difficulty into the conversation. How do you solve this problem?

4 Eating out

Before you listen

1 How often do you eat out? When you go to a restaurant, which of the following is most important to you?

- elegant surroundings   – efficient service   – good food
- romantic atmosphere   – lively atmosphere   – low prices

What other things can you add to this list?

2 Look at the three situations below.

1 A meal out with your husband/wife/boyfriend/girlfriend.
2 A meal with an important business client.
3 A celebration with a large group of colleagues from work.

Now put the things from the list in 1 in order of importance for you
(1 = most important) in the three situations.

3 Here are some words and phrases connected with eating. Which are *only* used for eating in a restaurant, and which can also be used for eating at home? Put R (Restaurant only) or R/H (Restaurant and Home) next to each.

to book a table	R	a menu	
a dessert	R/H	mineral water	
fully booked		to order a meal	
house wine		to pay the bill	
a main course		a starter	

Listening for information

JOANIE'S
Today's specials

Starters
Mediterranean Prawns
Vegetable Terrine
Fish Chowder

Main courses
Roast Lamb
Swordfish Steak
Vegetarian Lasagne
+full à la carte menu

T.4a

1 Paul works for a travel company in Oxford. To celebrate the birthday of a colleague, Paul and some of his workmates have decided to go to Joanie's, a restaurant near their office, for a meal. Listen to Paul telephoning the restaurant and complete the note below confirming his booking.

JOANIE'S Fully Licensed Restaurant and Wine Bar

Table booking

Date .... , ... *October*
Time
No. of people
Name   Tel. no.

T.4b

2 You will hear six short dialogues in the restaurant. The dialogues are in a different order from the list below. Listen and write the number of each dialogue next to the correct heading. Be careful: there are two extra headings. The first example has been done for you.

Arriving at the restaurant	___	Ordering more wine	___
Ordering starters	___	Deciding about the dessert	1
Ordering a main course	___	Asking for more coffee	___
Ordering something to drink	___	Asking for the bill	___

Listening for language

1 Look at the pairs of sentences below. One sentence is from the dialogues and in the other there is a mistake of grammar or style. Before you listen, look at them and decide which is right and which is wrong.

1 a. I like to book a table, please.
b. I'd like to book a table, please.

2 a. A table for four, please.
b. A table of four, please.

3 a. Could you tell me what is fish chowder?
b. Could you tell me what fish chowder is?

4 a. I have fish chowder then.
b. I'll have fish chowder then.

5 a. Please bring us a bottle of house white.
b. Could we have a bottle of house white, please?

6 a. Do you like a dessert?
b. Would you like a dessert?

7 a. Could we have some more coffee, please?
b. Could we have any more coffee, please?

8 a. Can we have our bill, please?
b. Would you mind to give us our bill, please?

T.4c 🔌○

2 Now listen and check your answers.

3 Practise saying the phrases you have heard. Copy the voices on the tape.

Speaking

1 Work in groups of three. Look at the menu below. Choose a name for your restaurant and add some dishes to the menu in the spaces marked (*).

Restaurant

MENU AT £13.50 (Including VAT)

Starters

Soup of the Day (served with French bread)

*

Home-made pâté (served with toast)

◀●▶

Main Courses

Chicken Kiev (breast of chicken stuffed with garlic butter and parsley)

*

12 oz. rump steak (£2.50 extra) (served with French fries, onion rings, and mushrooms)

Vegetables in season   Green / mixed salad

◀●▶

Desserts

Fruit salad

*

Chocolate gateau   Coffee 50p extra

◀●▶

Beverages

Wines	House White	£6.50
	Red	£6.50
Beers : draught or bottled (1/2 pint)		£1.20
Mineral water		£1.00
All spirits		£1.50

2 Still in groups of three, look at the information in the boxes below. Decide who will be the two diners, and who will be the waiter/waitress. After you have chosen your roles, choose from the prompts below.

Diners

You are | colleagues from work | having dinner at the restaurant.
a couple
business associates

You're both | not very hungry.
quite hungry.
very hungry.

One of you | is a vegetarian.
is on a diet.
doesn't drink alcohol.

You think the food is | excellent.
OK.
awful.

Waiter/Waitress

You're feeling | in a good mood, | so you're
very, very, tired,
very nervous (it's your first day!)

going to be | very polite.
a bit rude.

You're a | very good | waiter/waitress.
very bad

You want to | get a good tip.
go home as soon as possible.

---

3 Act out a conversation in the restaurant. After arriving at the restaurant, you order your starters, main courses, something to drink, a dessert/coffee, and then ask for the bill.

5 Shopping

1 In general, do you like shopping or not? Which of the things below do you most enjoy shopping for?

records   food   things for the house   furniture   books   presents for friends electrical items   clothes

Which of these things *don't* you like shopping for?

Do you prefer shopping alone or with someone else? Who do you usually go shopping with?

Is there anyone who you *dislike* shopping with? Why?

2 Look at the pictures of shops above and write the words in the box below under the correct picture.

a fitting room	re-heeling	a trim
a parcel	to fit someone	a jumper
a wash and blow dry	to suit someone	the medium size

Listening for information

T.5a

1 You will hear conversations taking place in the five shops. Listen and complete columns 1 and 2 below.

1 Which shop?	2 What does the customer want to buy?	3 How much does the customer pay?	4 What small problem is there?
a.			
b.			
c.			
d.			
e.			

T.5a

2 Listen again and complete columns 3 and 4.

Listening for language

1 Below is part of the conversation in the clothes shop. Put it in the correct order.

a. ☐ 'Erm . . . this jumper . . . Have you got this in a large?'

b. ☐ 'Does it fit OK?'

c. ☐ 'Thanks.'

d. ☐ 'No, I'm just looking, thanks.'

e. ☐ 'Can I help you at all?'

f. ☐ 'No, we've only got the small and the medium, but the sizes are quite big. Try it on – the fitting room's behind here . . . There you are.'

g. ☐ 'Yes, it fits perfectly, actually . . .'

h. ☐ 'Well, if you want anything, just give me a call . . .'

i. ☐ 10 'Mmm, I don't know about the colour, myself . . . This cream's going to get very dirty . . .'

j. ☐ 'Yes, it does. It looks really good on you. That colour suits you.'

| T.5b | ⌐—0 |

2 Listen and check your answers.

3 Practise reading the dialogue with a partner. Copy the voices on the tape.

Speaking

1 Look at the two lines of dialogue below and practise saying them with a partner.

> Have you got this one in black?

> I'm not sure. I'll have a look...

2 Look at the pictures. Decide what items of clothing you want to talk about and exactly what kind of shop you are in. Did the shop assistant or customer say anything before this? Practise the first part of the conversation.

3 Continue the conversation, thinking about these questions:

Customer	Shop assistant
– If they don't have it in black, what colour would you like instead? – Do you try it on? – Does it fit? – Do you like it? – Do you try anything else on? – Do you buy it? – How do you want to pay?	– Can you find the item in black? – Have you got it in any other colours or sizes? – How much does it cost? – Is it possible to pay by cheque or credit card?

Introduce at least one *problem* into the conversation. Practise the dialogue again.

4 Finally, decide about the *mood* of the shop assistant and customer.

Is the shop assistant	– good-tempered and friendly? – tired and bad-tempered? – *too* friendly and helpful?

Is the customer	– friendly and very talkative? – rude and snobbish? – a bit shy and embarrassed?

Practise the dialogue again, showing their moods clearly.

5 Act out your dialogue to the rest of the class. They should listen and say:

a. What you bought.
b. How much it cost and how you paid.
c. What mood you were both in.

6 On the phone

Discuss the following questions in pairs.

– Do you have a telephone at home? Who do you talk to most often? Do you ever have very long telephone conversations? What about the rest of your family?
– Do you or any of your friends have an answering machine? Have you ever had any problems with one?
– Have you ever made any telephone calls in English? Who did you speak to? Was it easy or difficult? Why?

Listening for information

Jayne is having a difficult day! She wants to go and see her family in Southampton this afternoon, but before she can leave, she has to make several phone calls. Read the list she has made.

*BR = British Rail (the national railway in Great Britain)

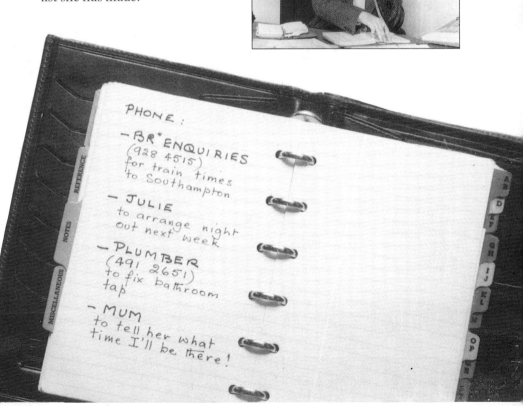

PHONE:

– BR* ENQUIRIES
(928 4515)
for train times
to Southampton

– JULIE
to arrange night
out next week

– PLUMBER
(491 2651)
to fix bathroom
tap

– MUM
to tell her what
time I'll be there!

T.6a   **1** Listen to the first two phone calls and choose the correct answers below.

a. The fast trains to Southampton in the afternoon leave
   ☐ every half hour.   ☐ every hour.   ☐ every two hours.

b. The journey takes
   ☐ less than an hour.   ☐ just over an hour.   ☐ about one and a
                                                      half hours.

c. Jayne tells Julie's colleague that
   ☐ Julie should ring   ☐ She (Jayne) will phone ☐ She'll see Julie on
      her back.   back later.   Monday.

d. Jayne's phone number is
   ☐ 692 4055.   ☐ 692 4050.   ☐ 692 4550.

Check your answers with a partner.

2 Listen to the next two calls and answer the questions below.

a. Who does Jayne speak to when she phones the plumber?
b. When did the plumber *say* that he would come to Jayne's house?
c. Who does Jayne speak to when she phones home?
d. What time does she expect to arrive home?

Check your answers with a partner.

Listening for language

1 Look at the extracts from Jayne's phone calls below. Can you fill in the gaps?

a. 'Hello. _____ you _____ me the train times to . . .'
b. 'Hello. Can I _____ extension 248, please?'
c. 'It's ringing for you . . .'
   'Hello, Marketing.'
   'Hello. _____ I speak _____ Julie Mitchell, please?'
d. 'Um . . . Could you _____ ____ a moment, please. I'll just check . . .'
e. 'She'll be busy for another hour or so . . . Can I _____ a _____ ?'
f. '_____ you _____ her that Jayne White _____ ?'
   'Jayne . . . White . . . OK?'
g. 'And could you _____ her to _____ me at home this afternoon,
   before four if she can?'
h. 'Hello? Is _____ JDT Plu-'
i. 'Yes. _____ is Jayne White. That's W-H-I-T-E . . .'
j. 'Oh, hi, Peter. ____ ____ . . .'
k. 'Is Mum _____ ?'

T.6b   Listen and check your answers.

2 All the phrases above are useful when you're talking on the telephone. But
   when would you use each one? Match the phrases with those in the chart
   opposite. The first example has been done for you.

1 Checking you've got the right number	h.	6 Asking to speak to someone (less formal)	__
2 Leaving a message	_ _	7 Saying who you are	_ _
3 Asking for information		8 Asking for an extension	__
4 Offering to take a message		9 Asking someone to wait	
5 Asking to speak to someone (formal)	__	10 Checking the information	_ _

3 Practise saying the expressions. Copy the voices on the tape.

Speaking

In pairs, look at the conversations below. Work out what you would say in each situation. Then act out the conversations.

1 Student B is telephoning a company to speak to the Export Manager.

Student A ☎	Student B ☎
1 (*telephonist*) Answer the phone (say the name of your company).	2 Ask for the Export Department (extention 280).
3 (*secretary*) Answer the phone (Hello?).	4 Check you've got the right extention.
5 Respond.	6 Ask to speak to the Export Manager.
7 Explain that the Export Manager is busy (she's in a meeting/at lunch, etc.)	8 Ask when she'll be back in the office.
9 You're not sure. Maybe tomorrow. Offer to take a message.	10 Leave a message (say who's calling, give your number, etc.).
11 Check that the details of the message are correct.	12 Listen and check that the details are correct. Say goodbye.
13 Say goodbye.	

2 This time you're phoning your friend, but his flatmate answers.

Student A ☎	Student B ☎
1 Answer the phone (Hello?).	2 Check you've got the right number.
3 Respond.	4 Say who you are.
5 Greet B. Say who you are.	6 Respond to A's greeting. Ask to speak to your friend.
7 Ask B to wait. You'll see if C's in.	8 Respond.
9 Your flatmate's gone out. Offer to take a message.	10 Give A a message. Say goodbye.
11 Say goodbye.	

Asking the way

1 If you have to find your way in a place you don't know very well, do you usually:

- ask someone on the street for directions?
- try to guess the way?
- go to a Tourist Information office?

- use a map?
- ask a policeman?
- get lost?

If you've ever been lost in a strange town, tell your partner about it. When/Where was it? What were you looking for? How did you try to find your way? How did you feel? Did you find your way in the end? How?

2 Where do you expect to see the places in the chart below?

1 An airport?   2 A street?   3 A school?

Put 1, 2, or 3 next to the places. Sometimes more than one is possible. The first has been done for you.

a library	2/3	a canteen	
a car hire office		a cemetery	
a staff room		a corridor	
a staircase		a hospital	
a bus stop		a church	
a Bureau de Change		an arrivals lounge	

3 Now look at the maps opposite and find the places on them.

Listening for information

T.7a

1 You will now hear three conversations in which people are asking the way. Choose the best summary of each conversation.

a. The young woman directs the man to the Bureau de Change.
b. The young woman directs the man to the car hire office.
c. The young woman tells the man where the shops are.

T.7b

a. The man tells the young couple how to get to a hotel outside the centre of town.
b. The man tells the young couple how to get to a nearby hotel on foot.
c. The man tells the young couple how to get to the bus stop.

T.7c

a. The receptionist directs a student to her classroom.
b. The receptionist directs a student to the ladies' toilets.
c. The receptionist tells someone where she can find a teacher.

2 Look at the three maps and listen again. Decide in each conversation if they are talking about the places marked A, B, C, or D.

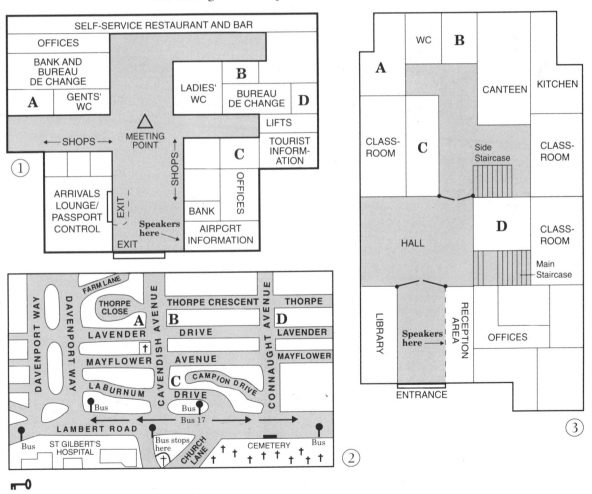

Listening for language

1   Look at the following extracts from the dialogues. Underline the correct word or phrase. The first one has been done for you.

   a. Is there somewhere here where *can I*/ *I can* hire a car?

   b. You go straight *in*/*on* past these shops. . .

   c. . . . It's *next*/*next to* the Bureau de Change.

   d. How do we *get*/*go* there?

   e. . . . Then you walk *up*/*along* there for about 200 metres.

   f. . . . The Dolphin's just there, *at*/*on* the right-hand corner of Lavender Drive and Cavendish Avenue.

   g. Can you *say*/*tell* me where the staff room is?

   h. Yes, you go *through*/*to* this set of doors here.

   i. *Go past*/*Pass* the main staircase . . .

T.7d ⬛▬0

2   Now listen to the extracts and check your answers.

   Practise saying the expressions. Copy the voices on the tape.

Speaking

1   Work in pairs. Student A read card 1 below.
   Student B read card 2 on page 72. Using the maps on page 31, ask for and give the necessary directions.

   > **Card 1**
   > 1 You are at the airport information desk (map 1) and want to know where the telephones are.
   > 2 You are at the bus stop opposite the hospital (map 2) and want to know the way to the George Hotel.
   > 3 You are at the reception desk in the school and want to know where the Director's office is.
   > _____
   >
   > *Answers to B's questions*
   > – the flower shop is A on map 1.
   > – the Park Gates Hotel is A on map 2 (you are at the bus stop opposite the hospital).
   > – the computer centre is B on map 3.

   Which place (A, B, C, or D) did your partner direct you to each time?

2   Think of a place that you and your partner both know, but *don't* tell your partner what it is. (The place can be either inside your school, or outside in the town.) Direct your partner there from where you are now. Can your partner say what the place is?

8 Booking in to a hotel

1 Here are four pairs of words connected with hotels.
Is there any difference in meaning between the words in each pair?

ground floor	a lift	a bath	a twin room
first floor	an elevator	a shower	a single room

2 Work in pairs. Discuss the following questions:

– How often do you stay in hotels? Have you ever stayed in a really good/really bad hotel?
– Imagine a visitor is coming to stay in your town/city. Which hotel would you recommend? Why?
– Would you like to be a hotel receptionist? What qualities are important in this job?

Listening for information

1 Philip is a student living in a small flat in Cambridge. One day, he receives a letter from his mother, who lives in York, in the north-east of England. Read part of her letter and answer the following questions:
– What is Philip's mother planning to do?
– What does she want Philip to do?

and since your father will be away that week, I thought I'd take the opportunity to come and see you in Cambridge.
Perhaps you could book me in to a hotel – something reasonably comfortable, with a bath, and on the ground floor, so I don't have any stairs to climb.
So, I'll be coming down to Cambridge on

T.8a

2 Philip telephones a nearby hotel to make a reservation for his mother. Listen to his conversation with the hotel receptionist, and fill in the details of his booking below.

⏛ QUEENS HOTEL

Name MR MRS MS MISS	Initials	Type of room	Price	Date of arrival	Date of departure	Address Tel. home / work

🔑

T.8b

3 Mrs Beaumont arrives at the hotel . . . but not everything is as she wanted. Listen to her conversation with the hotel receptionist, and make short notes about the three problems mentioned. How does the receptionist deal with them?

Problem	Solution
1	1
2	2
3	3

🔑

**Listening for
language**

1 Here are some of the phrases Philip and the receptionist used in their
telephone conversation. Put the words into the correct order.

a. like/to/reservation/make/a/please/I'd

_____

b. nights/for/It's/three/the 28th/the 26th/to/from

_____

c. price/tell/you/the/me/Could/please?

_____

d. name/I/have/Can/please/the?

_____

e. you/like/for/When/reservation/the/would?

_____

f. single/room/a/double/that/a/Is/or?

_____

T.8c 🔌 2 Listen to the extracts and check your answers.

Speaking

Look at the information about the Cotswold Lodge Hotel on page 36. With a
partner, make up a dialogue using the prompts below.

Student A
You are telephoning the Cotswold Lodge Hotel to book a room.
First think about the following questions:
When do you want the room?
How long do you want the room for?
Do you want a single/double/bath/shower, etc?

What questions will you ask to find out the following information?
– the _price_ of the room
– how to get to the hotel
– what time you can have dinner

Student B

You work as a receptionist at the Cotswold Lodge Hotel. Look at the information, and be ready to give Student A the following information:
– the price of different types of rooms
– how to get to the hotel
– what time dinner is available

What questions will you ask to find out the following information?
– the caller's name/address/telephone number, etc.
– the type of room he or she wants (double/single/with bath/shower)
– when he or she wants the room, and for how many nights

Practise your conversation with your partner.

Cotswold Lodge Hotel
Oxford

In the city of Oxford there is a small private hotel that has those qualities which set it apart from others: the 3 Star Cotswold Lodge Hotel. It is rich in atmosphere and provides tourists and businesspeople with the ideal location, only half a mile from the centre of Oxford, and yet set in a quiet conservation area.

The 52 bedrooms offer not only comfort but a variety of style and size. In addition to the delightful furnishings each bedroom has a private bathroom, colour television, telephone, and hairdrier.

All rooms have en suite bathroom.
Rates include full English breakfast and VAT.

Lunch *served daily*	12.00-2.30pm	
Dinner *served nightly*	6.30-10.30pm	
Table d'hôte and full à la carte menus		
Bar snacks *also available*		

We cater for conferences, banquets and wedding receptions for up to 150 people.

All enquiries welcome.

Single	per night	£79.50
Double/twin	per night	£102.50
Treble	per night	£125.50

Dinner, bed, and breakfast

Single	per night	£97.50
Double/twin	per night	£135.50
Treble	per night	£172.50

Special weekend rates (Friday–Sunday)

	2 nights	3 nights
Single	£110.00	£159.00
Double/twin	£143.00	£210.00
Treble	£170.00	£250.00

Dinner, bed, and breakfast (weekend)

	2 nights	3 nights
Single	£145.00	£212.00
Double/twin	£200.00	£298.00
Treble	£265.00	£390.00

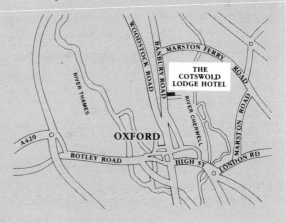

9 Looking for somewhere to live

Before you listen

1   Imagine that you have to move to another city to work or study for a couple of years. The first thing you have to do is to find somewhere to live. You decide in the end to rent a flat. Do the quiz below to find out the best kind of accommodation for you.

Lifestyle quiz

1 Would you prefer to

a. live alone? ☐
b. share with just one friend or colleague? ☐
c. share with a group of other people? ☐

2 Which of the following would you prefer?

a. a fully-furnished flat ☐
b. a flat with a little basic furniture ☐
c. an unfurnished flat ☐

3 What is your attitude to money?

a. You want to find somewhere as cheap as possible. ☐
b. You want to be careful about money, but it's also important to live somewhere nice. ☐
c. You don't care how much you pay – you want to live in luxury! ☐

4 Would you choose to live

a. in the city centre, close to all the shops, cinemas, etc? ☐
b. in a nice suburb, not too far from the centre? ☐
c. in the countryside outside the city? ☐

5 Which six of the following would be the most important to you?

- cleanliness and tidiness ☐
- being near the shops ☐
- good public transport ☐
- low bills ☐
- being on the ground floor ☐
- having your own room ☐
- a telephone ☐
- a garden ☐
- a balcony ☐
- parking space for your car ☐
- a washing machine ☐

2   Work in pairs. Close your book and describe to your partner your ideal accommodation, using your answers to the questions in 1.

Listening for information

1 In Britain it is very common for young people to share flats, because it is so expensive to buy one. Read about Annie, who is hoping to share a flat in London.

Annie is twenty-two. She has just left university, and is moving to London to start her first job. She has decided to look in the newspaper to try to find a room in a shared house or flat. She is looking for something in West London, and doesn't want to pay more than about £60 a week. Ideally, she would like to share with young men and women, as she doesn't have many friends in London and would like to meet some new people.

2 Annie has only found four suitable advertisements in her newspaper. Which one(s) do you think would be best for her?

1

WEST KENSINGTON W14
Single rooms in large flat with two bathrooms, shower, central heating, washing machine, drier, newly decorated for young professionals, close to Underground. £55 to £60 per week.
071 381 9875 or 071 683 3737.

3

BARNES SW13 Non-smoker to share with 2 others in comfortable house: large room, double bed, fully furnished throughout, all modern conveniences, 2 minutes to shops, 5 minutes to B.R.* £250 per calendar month excluding bills, plus deposit. Phone Andrew 071 936 5555 ext 4402 or 071 439 5124.

* B.R.=British Rail station
(national railways in Britain)

2

EALING W5 Male or female for own room in large friendly shared house. Gas central heating, shower, separate toilet. Near Ealing Common tube station. £61 per week excluding bills, plus one month's deposit. 071 465 1493 days 9–5.30 p.m. or 081 579 8118 after 6.30 and weekends.

4

EALING W5 Female to share with two others. Own room in clean house. Central heating, washing machine, etc. Close to tube and B.R. £240 per month including bills. Phone 081 798 8871 after 6.00.

T.9a

3 Annie decides to phone about all four advertisements. Listen and answer the questions below.

   a. Which of the rooms does she arrange to see?
   b. When does she arrange to see them?
   c. Why doesn't she arrange to see the other rooms?

T.9a

4 Listen to conversations 3 and 4 again and complete Annie's notes below.

	Room itself	Rent / bills	Transport / local area	Other people living there	Address
Barnes		✕			15 Grove Road
Ealing	– large – not much furniture – nice		✕	– Linda – Sophie (away a lot)	

Listening for language

1 Below is part of conversation 4. Can you put the sentences in the correct order? The first one has been done for you.

   a. ☐ 'Yes, it is.'
   b. ☐ 'That's right, gas and electricity are included. The telephone bill's separate, though.'
   c. ☐ 'I see. And who else lives in the flat?'
   d. ☐1 'Hello.'
   e. ☐ 'And that's with bills, isn't it?'
   f. ☐ 'Could you tell me something about it?'
   g. ☐ 'Certainly!'
   h. ☐ 'Hello, I'm phoning about the room you advertised. Is it still available?'
   i. ☐ 'Well, there's me. My name's Linda, by the way, and the other person is Sophie, but she's away quite a lot because she travels with her job . . .'
   j. ☐ 'Right . . . well, would it be possible for me to come and see it?'
   k. ☐ 'Well, I think most of the information is in the advert. It's quite a large room. There's not much furniture, but it's very nice. It's £240 a month . . .'

T.9b

2 Listen and check your answers.

3 Practise reading the dialogue with a partner. (See tapescript on page 68.)

Speaking

Annie decides to phone Richard Gray, from the first advertisement, later in the day. With a partner, act out their conversation, using some of the expressions from the dialogues. Student A is Annie, Student B is Richard. Before you start, decide the answers to the questions below.

Annie

– What questions will you ask about the flat?
– When are you free to go and see the flat?

Richard

– What *extra* information can you give Annie about the flat that is not in the advertisement?
– Do you live there yourself?
– Who else lives there?
– When are you free to show Annie the flat?

Meeting new people

1 In your country, when you meet friends in the street, do you shake hands, kiss, or just say hello? What about when you are introduced to new people? Is this the same in other countries that you know?

2 Presently you will hear a conversation between Chris, his girlfriend Fran, and his parents, Mr and Mrs Hunt. Fran and Chris, who met at university in Canterbury, have been going out together for eight months. Chris has brought Fran home to meet his parents, who live in Leeds. They have come by car.

How do you think Fran and Chris feel just before they arrive?
What about Mr and Mrs Hunt? What sort of things do you think they will talk about when they first meet?

Listening for information

T.10

1 Listen and tick (√) the things that the people mention.

the weather

the Hunt's house and garden

the cat

food

tea

Fran's studies

Fran's family

coffee

Chris and Fran's journey to Leeds

the dog

◄ T.10

2 Listen again and answer the questions below.

a. Before Fran and Chris arrive, what does Mrs Hunt tell Mr Hunt to do?

_____

b. What kind of dog is Sammy, according to Mrs Hunt?

_____

c. What time did Fran and Chris start their journey?

_____

d. What does Fran say about the Hunts' home?

_____

e. What subjects is Fran studying at university?

_____

f. What job would she like to do after she finishes university?

_____

g. Why doesn't Fran want anything to eat?

_____

h. What does Chris want to eat?

_____

3 Did the four people act as you expected? Did anyone seem shy or nervous, do you think?

_____

Listening for language

1 Who said the things below? Who to?

a.
> Hello, darling.
> Lovely to see you!

Mrs Hunt to Chris

g.
> Let me take your coat, dear.

_____

b.
> Hi, Mum!

_____

h.
> This is my husband.

_____

c.
> Let me introduce you to Fran.

_____

i.
> Delighted to meet you!

_____

d.
> Fran—Mum...

_____

j.
> Do sit down and make yourself comfortable.

_____

e.
> How do you do.

_____

k.
> What was your journey like?

_____

f.
> It's so nice to meet you at last.

_____

l.
> You must be starving!

_____

◄ T.10 **2** Listen and check your answers.

3 Do any of the phrases above sound more formal or informal than the others?

4 What is the answer to e.?

Speaking

1   Practise saying the phrases in 1. Copy the voices on the tape.

2   Work in groups of three or four. Look at the photographs below. In each photograph, one person is being introduced to the others. Which person is it? Who is introducing them?

1

2

3

4

5

Each group choose one picture. You are going to act out the conversation, and each person in the group will be one of the people in the photograph.

First, decide the answers to the following questions:
- What is the relationship between the people?
- Where exactly are they?
- What time of day is it?
- Why is this person being introduced to the others?
- Is there any special reason?
- How does each person feel? Is anyone shy or nervous? Is anyone particularly talkative?
- What kind of thing will they talk about, to make conversation? What kind of questions will they ask?

Practise your conversation and try to include some of the expressions you have heard.
Then act it out to the rest of the class. They try to work out which picture you chose.

11 At the doctor's

1   In the box are some words and phrases connected with being ill. Write them in the chart under A or B.

take your temperature	take antibiotics
have an ear infection	have a sore throat
go to the surgery	pay a prescription charge
have a headache	aches and pains
get a prescription	go to the chemist's
have earache	a virus

A Medical problems	**B What you do when you're ill**
_____	_____
_____	_____
_____	_____
_____	_____
_____	_____

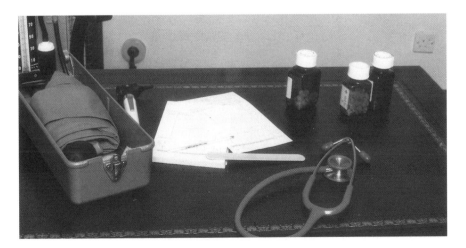

2 Daniel, who comes from Germany, is staying with friends in Manchester. One day, he felt ill and had to see a doctor. The sentences below describe what happened. What order do you think they happened in? The first one has been done for you.

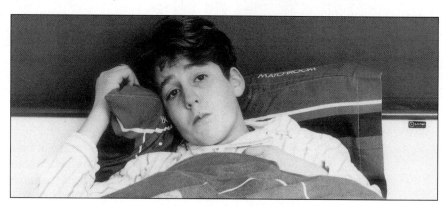

He went to the doctor's surgery.	
The doctor wrote a prescription.	
Daniel paid a prescription charge at the chemist's.	
Daniel woke up with a sore throat and earache.	1
The doctor told him he had an ear infection.	
Daniel told the doctor what was wrong.	
Daniel took the paracetamol and antibiotics.	
Daniel spoke to the receptionist.	
He felt better.	
Daniel filled in a form.	
He saw the doctor.	

Listening for information

T.11a

1 You will hear Daniel speaking to the doctor's receptionist. Listen and tick (√) the statements which are true.

  a. Daniel was sent to Dr Graham's surgery by some friends. ☐
  b. His friends are also patients there. ☐
  c. He has been staying with his friends for several months. ☐
  d. Before he can see the doctor, Daniel has to fill in a special form. ☐
  e. He has to come back another day. ☐
  f. He doesn't have to pay anything. ☐

2 If the statements are *not* true, say why.

T.11b

3 Daniel then goes in to see the doctor. Listen to their conversation and put the pictures below into the correct order.

a. b. c. d. e. f. g. h.

Listening for language

1 Below are some things that a patient might say to a doctor, and some things that a doctor might say to a patient. Put D next to the things a doctor would say, and P next to the things a patient would say. The first one has been done for you.

a. **P** 'I've been feeling unwell for a few days.'
b. ☐ 'You should go to bed for a couple of days.'
c. ☐ 'Have plenty of hot drinks.'
d. ☐ 'I think I've got a temperature.'
e. ☐ 'I've got a bad headache.'
f. ☐ 'Keep warm.'
g. ☐ 'Just eat very light food.'
h. ☐ 'I've been vomiting a lot.'

i. ☐ 'I've got aches and pains all over.'
j. ☐ 'I've got a very sore throat.'
k. ☐ 'Try to relax more.'
l. ☐ 'I've got really bad earache.'
m. ☐ 'I'm going to give you some antibiotics.'
n. ☐ 'Take one of these tablets four times a day.'
o. ☐ 'I've got stomachache.'
p. ☐ 'Take paracetamol for the headache.'

◀ T.11b

2 Which of these sentences did Daniel say, and which did Dr Graham say? Listen again and check your answers.

3 Practise saying the sentences that Daniel and Dr Graham used. Copy the voices on the tape.

Speaking

1   Match the pictures to the illnesses. Then look at the sentences on page 47 again. What might a patient say to the doctor if he or she had these illnesses?

| flu (influenza) | food poisoning | stress/exhaustion |

What might the doctor say to the patient?

2   Work in pairs.

Student A You're ill. Describe what's wrong to the doctor.

Student B You're the doctor. Ask A questions and give your advice.

12 Looking for a job

1 In your country do students ever do part-time or holiday jobs to earn extra money? What kind of jobs do they usually do? Have you ever done this kind of 'casual' work? What was it like?

All of the jobs below could be casual jobs. Which would you *least* enjoy? Which would you enjoy the *most*, do you think? Why?

working as a waiter	bar work	babysitting
cleaning	fruit picking	factory work
working in a bookshop	working in a supermarket	selling ice-cream

2 All the words below relate to work. Match the words in **A** with the definitions in **B**.

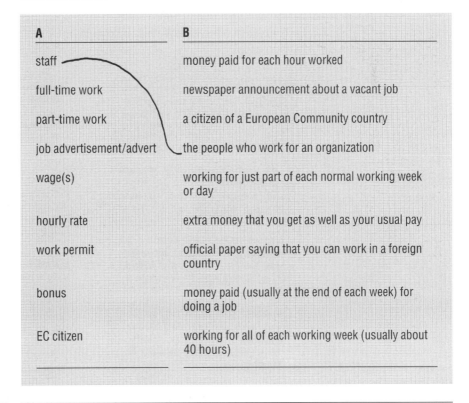

A	B
staff	money paid for each hour worked
full-time work	newspaper announcement about a vacant job
part-time work	a citizen of a European Community country
job advertisement/advert	the people who work for an organization
wage(s)	working for just part of each normal working week or day
hourly rate	extra money that you get as well as your usual pay
work permit	official paper saying that you can work in a foreign country
bonus	money paid (usually at the end of each week) for doing a job
EC citizen	working for all of each working week (usually about 40 hours)

Listening for information

Max is a Dutch student who has been studying at Art College in Britain. He is in the college coffee bar talking to his friend, Rachel, about his plans for the summer.

19A 20 20A 21 21A 22 22A

T.12a

1 Listen to the first part of their conversation and look at the topics below. Tick (√) the ones that they talk about. The first one has been done for you.

exams √	work permits
Max's money problems	rates of pay in Britain
Max's problems with his parents	how to look for a job
the type of job that Max would like	job interviews

What do they say about these things?

2 Look at the job advertisements below. What work does the person have to do in each case?

a. **Sandwich makers required.** Sunday 7 a.m. to 11 a.m., Monday to Thursday 6 a.m. to 10 a.m. Wage £2.50 per hour. Call 665439 mornings only.

b. **Taxi company** urgently requires owner-drivers. Reliable day, night, and weekend drivers needed. Phone 654545 and ask for Tony.

c. **Lucani Brothers Ice-Cream.** Staff required to sell hot dogs, ice-cream, and hamburgers. Call 754433 daytime and 828113 evenings.

d. **Spanish restaurant** requires chef and assistant bar staff. Couple considered. Write to D. Anderson, 56 Ruskin House, Selsdon Rd, South Croxby.

e. **Reception bar** vacancies in busy central night club. Good rates of pay, taxi home, meal provided. Hours 8.30 p.m. to 2.30 a.m. Call Jean or Jane on 589032.

f. **Lunchtime help** wanted in sandwich bar in Chipstead near Coulsdon. 11 a.m. to 2 p.m. Mon-Fri £3 p.h. Hard worker with a sense of humour essential. **Call Richard on 789860.**

g. **Part-time cook** required to serve light meals for up to eight persons every Friday lunchtime. Kitchen equipment available. Pay by agreement. Contact Mrs Anne Kent on 587878.

h. **Domestic cleaners** required, part time, £3 p.h. Tel 652221

T.12b

Listen to the second part of the conversation between Max and Rachel and answer the questions below.

a. Which four adverts do Max and Rachel discuss?_____

b. Which two is Max interested in? _____

c. Why doesn't he want to do the other two jobs that they discuss?

_____

_____

T.12c

3 Listen to Max telephoning about one of the jobs. Which of the notes below does he write for himself after the phone call?

a.
```
8.30 – 2.30
(meal / taxi)
3.15 per hour + bonus
(no uniform)

112 Brighton Road,
Purley.

Ask for Jane.
```

b.
```
8.30 – 2.30
(meal / taxi)
3.50 per hour (+ bonus)
UNIFORM

112 Brighton Road,
Purley.

Ask for Jane.
```

c.
```
8.30 – 2.30
(meal / taxi)
2.50 per hour
(wear uniform)

120 Brighton Road,
Purley.

Ask for Jane.
```

Listening for language

1 Below is the first part of the last conversation. Try to fill in the gaps.

I'm _____ _____ your advertisement for reception and bar staff in the *Evening Telegraph.*

Yes.

Can you _____ ____ _____ _____ the bar job?

I think most of the details are ____ ____ ____ . It's 8.30 to 2.30. There's a meal provided and a _____ _____ if you need one. The _____ ____ is £3.50 _____ _____ , and bar staff____ __ ____ .

What do I do if I want ____ _____ ?

T.12d 🔑

2 Listen and check your answers.

Practise the dialogue with a partner. Copy the voices on the tape.

Speaking

Work in pairs.
Student A You are telephoning about one of the advertisements on page 50. Decide what questions you will ask.
Student B You answer the phone. Decide what answers to give to A's questions. Are you going to ask any questions yourself?

13 Using machines

a.
b.
c.
d.

e.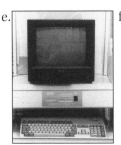
f.
g.
h.
i.

Before you listen

1 Write in the English words for the machines in the pictures. Which of them do you have at home? Do you know how to use them? Have you ever had any problems using them?

2 Which of the words in the box go with the machines? Often more than one is possible. The first one has been done for you.

channel TV	to plug in
dial	to press a button
disk	to record
drawer	screen
file	to switch on/off
menu	

⌐─0

53

Listening for information

T.13

1 You will hear three short dialogues in which people are talking about different machines. Listen to the dialogues and complete the chart below.

Relationship between speakers	Machine being discussed
1	1
2	2
3	3

2 Listen again and answer the following questions.

1a. How much washing powder does Mrs Bolton use for a normal wash?
 b. Which programme does she normally use?
 c. Why doesn't she usually use the drier?

2a. Has the man tried to use the video recorder before?
 b. What kind of programme does he want to record?
 c. When does the programme start/finish?

3a. How does the grandfather feel about computers?
 b. How does the grandson feel about them?
 c. What does the grandfather do at the end?

3 Which person is perhaps *annoyed* in each conversation? Why?

Listening for language

1 Match a question in **A** with an answer in **B**.

A	B
1 How does it work exactly?	a. Nothing. You just have to wait for a minute.
2 What's this dial for?	b. You lose the file.
3 Why's it doing that?	c. It's really very simple. I'll show you.
4 What if I want to record another programme?	d. Well, you just press this button here and you do the same thing again.
5 Nothing's happening! What's wrong with it?	e. That's for the drier.
6 What happens if I press this?	f. I don't know ... What've you done to it?

2 Listen and check your answers.

3 Practise the questions in 1. Copy the voices on the tape.

Speaking
Have you got a machine with you? (A Walkman? A camera? A calculator?) Explain how it works to your partner. He or she should ask as many questions as possible, so that you both really know how to use it!

Saying goodbye

1 Look at the photographs. Why are these people at the station, do you think? How do they know each other? What kind of things are they saying to each other?

2 Read the information about the four people in the photographs. Check the meaning of anything you don't understand.

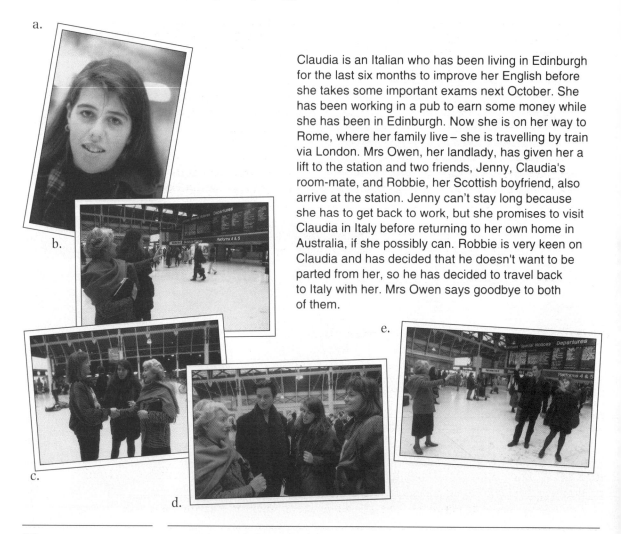

a.

b.

Claudia is an Italian who has been living in Edinburgh for the last six months to improve her English before she takes some important exams next October. She has been working in a pub to earn some money while she has been in Edinburgh. Now she is on her way to Rome, where her family live – she is travelling by train via London. Mrs Owen, her landlady, has given her a lift to the station and two friends, Jenny, Claudia's room-mate, and Robbie, her Scottish boyfriend, also arrive at the station. Jenny can't stay long because she has to get back to work, but she promises to visit Claudia in Italy before returning to her own home in Australia, if she possibly can. Robbie is very keen on Claudia and has decided that he doesn't want to be parted from her, so he has decided to travel back to Italy with her. Mrs Owen says goodbye to both of them.

e.

c.

d.

3 Work with a partner. How much can your partner remember about the four people in the pictures? Think of some questions to ask your partner:
– Where is Claudia from?
– How long has she been in Edinburgh?

Listening for information

T.14

1 Listen to the conversation between Claudia and her friends. There are five differences between the information on page 56 and the information in the conversation. Underline the differences on page 56.

2 Compare your answers with your partner's.

Listening for language

1 Can you remember who said the following?

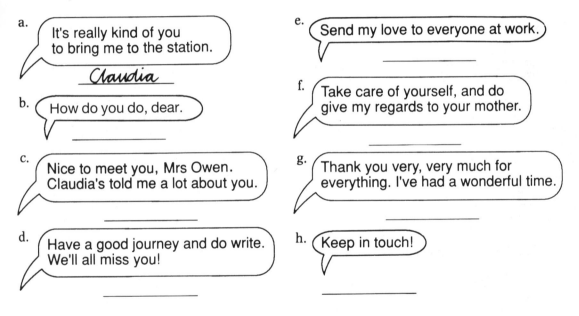

a. It's really kind of you to bring me to the station.
Claudia

b. How do you do, dear. _____

c. Nice to meet you, Mrs Owen. Claudia's told me a lot about you. _____

d. Have a good journey and do write. We'll all miss you! _____

e. Send my love to everyone at work. _____

f. Take care of yourself, and do give my regards to your mother. _____

g. Thank you very, very much for everything. I've had a wonderful time. _____

h. Keep in touch! _____

T.14

2 Listen again and check your answers.

3 Discuss these questions in pairs.

1 Which sentences in 1 above are connected with *saying hello*, *saying goodbye*, and *saying thank you*?

2 What is the answer to each one? First think of some possible answers, then look at the tapescript on page 72.

3 Which expressions seem more formal? Why is this, do you think?

4 Practise the expressions above, together with their answers.

Speaking

Work in groups of four.

Either

Imagine that one of you is going away for a long time. The others have all come to say goodbye to you. Act out your conversation. Before you start, decide the answers to the following questions:

– Where are you? (at the airport, the station, a café, home?)
– Why is your friend going away?
– How long is he or she going for?
– When will each of you see him or her again?

Or

Each person chooses one of the cards below. You are the person on the card.

GEORGE

You are a student studying English at a language school in Brighton, England. You are now returning to your home town because you have to start your new job in a big local hotel. You have had a wonderful time in Britain.

ANDY

You are George's English flatmate, who has driven him to the airport – to say goodbye to him. You hope to visit him in his home town next Christmas if you can save enough money. You already know Alison very well, but not Mr Hamilton.

MR HAMILTON

You are an old friend of George's father. You have come to the airport to say goodbye to George and to give him some presents for the family. You hope to see George and his family next summer when you are in their town on business. You have never met Andy or Alison before.

ALISON

You are George's English girlfriend. You have known him for six months and are very upset he is leaving. You arrive a bit late at the airport because you have been working. You hope to visit George in two months' time if you can get holidays from work.

Act out the four people's conversation.

Tapescript section

Unit 1

Tapescript 1a

D: David **R:** Ray

D 487533 – David Carr speaking.

R Hi, David, it's Ray, Ray Lewis. I'm calling from New York. . .

D Ray! I can't believe it! How are you?

R I'm great. . . Listen I have to talk fast – you don't know how much this is costing! You remember you said if I ever came to England to give you a call. . .

D Yeah, sure. . .

R Well, I'm coming over to England next week, so I was wondering . . .

D What!

R Yeah – I'm coming over! Just for a few days on my way to Italy to see my girlfriend. . .

D Well that's . . . er . . . great – so when are you coming?

R Next Friday, that's the 21st. . . Listen, would it be OK if I stayed over with you for a couple of days? You did say any time. . .

D Yeah, sure, no problem. Next Friday, you say?

R That's right. Listen, I'm flying in to Heathrow, arriving at . . . er . . . 8.30 in the morning your time. . . Can you meet me somewhere?

D Mmm . . . Next Friday's a bit difficult. You see, I'm working till about six – so I really can't get up to London. . .

R Don't worry. I can get from Heathrow to Brighton, no problem.

D Are you sure?

R Yeah, I'm sure! If you can just tell me how to get there, because I don't really know London. . .

D Of course. Listen, have you got a pen?

R I'll just go and get one. . .

Tapescript 1b

R OK. I'm ready.

D Right. The best thing is to get the Underground from Heathrow into London – it's the Piccadilly Line. You can get that right into the centre of town. Just look for the Underground sign at the airport.

R The Piccadilly Line, OK. So where do I catch that to?

D You take the Piccadilly Line as far as Green Park.

R Green . . . Park.

D That'll take you about three-quarters of an hour. . .

R Three-quarters of an hour! I'll remember to take a book!

D Yes, it's quite a long journey. Well, from Green Park you want to get to Victoria Station – the British Rail station. You can get a train from there to Brighton.

R Right, so how do I get to Victoria from Green Park?

D Well, you either change lines on the Underground or catch a bus.

R Yeah? I think I'll get a bus . . . It's years since I was on one of those double-deckers, and I won't have too much luggage.

D OK, so you want a number 38 or a 25. They both go to Victoria. . .

R . . . 38 or 25, OK . . . and that's from right outside the station?

D No, you have to cross the road. That's important, or you'll be going the wrong way. . . The bus stop's exactly opposite the station, as far as I remember. . .

R Well I can ask someone. . . So I get to Victoria. What next?

D Well, there are lots of trains from Victoria to Brighton – about three or four an hour, so you won't have to wait long. . . Just look at the departures board. . . If you're lucky you'll get the fast train which leaves at six minutes past the hour. . .

R And how long's that going to take? From Victoria?

D The fast ones take less than an hour, I think. . . The normal ones are about an hour and a quarter. . .

R Oh, well that's not bad. . .

D Listen, why don't you give me a ring from Victoria, if you have time, so that I have some idea of what time you'll be here?

R OK, I'll do that if I can. . .

D And the best thing is probably to get a taxi from Brighton station. . . I'm sorry I can't come to meet you . . . but it's not far from there to the office, and I'll be there all afternoon . . . you've got the address, haven't you?

R Somewhere, yeah. . .

D Well, write it down again, just in case . . . it's Davis International, 55, Seaview Road . . . that's S-E-A-V-I-E-W.

R OK, I've got it. . .

D Right. . . Are you sure you won't get lost?

R Trust me, OK! I'll be there! And thanks a lot, David.

D Well, I'm really looking forward to seeing you.

Tapescript 1c

1 Any more fares, please. . . ? Any more fares, please. . . ?

2 We apologize for the late departure of the 10.06 service to Brighton.

3 Stand clear of the doors, please. . . Let the passengers off first, please. . . Stand clear of the doors.

4 Platform 15 for the 10.32 service to Brighton, calling at Clapham Junction, East Croydon, Redhill, Gatwick Airport, Three Bridges. . .

5 Where do you want me to drop you?

6 Excuse me, is this the right train for Brighton?

7 It's OK, you can keep the change.

8 Excuse me, can you tell me where I can catch a bus to Victoria, please?

9 Excuse me, is this seat free?

10 One to Victoria, please.

Unit 2

Tapescript 2a

C: Cindy   **A:** Aileen

C More wine?

A Mmm, yes please. . .

C I must say it's really great to see you again. . . Anyway, how long are you going to be in London?

A I'll be here till Sunday – the conference finishes on Saturday about 5.00, so I thought I'd stay and go back the next day.

C Oh, really, that long? So, will you be free on Saturday night, then?

A Well, I haven't got anything planned. . .

C Then let's do something special, shall we? Since it's your last night. . .

A Yeah, that's a great idea! What do you fancy doing?

C No, *you* choose – I'm in London all the time.

A Mmm . . . OK, then . . . let me think . . . actually what I *really* wanted to do while I was here was to go to the theatre . . . see a musical maybe . . .

C Yeah, why not? Why don't we get tickets for something really good. . .

A How about *Miss Saigon?* Have you seen that?

C No I haven't.

A I'd really love to see it – I've heard it's brilliant!

C Mmm, the problem is, it's probably really difficult to get tickets.

A Well we can try, can't we?

C Sure. Let's have a look in the paper and see what it says. Oh, yes. It gives the number of a ticket agency – Ticketmaster . . . I'll give them a ring.

A Great!

C And in case they haven't got tickets for *Miss Saigon*, is there anything else you'd like to see?

A Well, I've heard that *Starlight Express* is quite good. I wouldn't mind seeing that.

C Right, well, we'll see. I'll try them tomorrow. Anyway, you still haven't told me any of your news – what about this new boyfriend – What's his name . . . Angus, isn't it?

Tapescript 2b

C: Cindy   **RM:** Recorded message   **O:** Operator

RM Thank you for calling Ticketmaster. All the lines are busy at the moment, but an operator will be with you shortly, so please have your . . .

O Hello, Ticketmaster.

C Oh, er yes. . . I'd like to know if you have tickets for *Miss Saigon* for this weekend, if possible. . .

O I'm afraid there are no tickets available for the next three months at the moment.

C Three months!

O No, sorry, there's nothing till July at least.

C Oh, well that's a bit late. . . I was hoping for something for this week.

O No, as I said, there's nothing for the next three months.

C Oh well, never mind. . . How about *Starlight Express?* Do you have anything for that?

O When would that be for?

C Well, for Saturday, if that's possible.

O I'll just check for you.

O Hello. Yes, we do have some tickets available for Saturday. Would you like the matinee or the evening performance?

C Oh, the evening please, if that's possible. Could you tell me the price, please?

O Well, we have tickets at eleven pounds, fourteen pounds fifty, and eighteen pounds fifty, and there is a five pound booking fee to pay in addition to that.
Ah, I'm afraid the tickets at fourteen pounds fifty are sold out, so it's either the eleven pound ones or the eighteen pound fifty ones.

C Um . . . I think eighteen fifty's a bit. . . Well, what's the difference?

O The eighteen fifty ones are in the stalls . . . the eleven pound tickets are in the dress circle and we only have a few left.

C Oh, I see... Well ... yes, it'll have to be the eleven pound ones, I think.

O OK. And how many tickets would you like?

C Two, please.

O Mm ... there are two in Row C ... numbers five and six ... they're not too near the side.

C OK, fine.

O Right, and how would you like to pay?

Tapescript 2c

C: Cindy   **A:** Aileen

C More wine?

A Mmm, yes please...

C I must say it's really great to see you again... Anyway, how long are you going to be in London?

A I'll be here till Sunday – the conference finishes on Saturday about 5.00, so I thought I'd stay and go back the next day.

C Oh, really, that long? So, will you be free on Saturday night, then?

A Well, I haven't got anything planned...

C Then let's do something special, shall we? Since it's your last night...

A Yeah, that's a great idea! What do you fancy doing?

C No, *you* choose – I'm in London all the time.

A Mmm... OK, then ... let me think ... actually what I *really* wanted to do while I was here was to go to the theatre ... see a musical maybe...

C Yeah, why not? Why don't we get tickets for something really good...

A How about *Miss Saigon*? Have you seen that?

Unit 3

Tapescript 3a

C: Claire   **T:** Tim   **B:** Barman

C So what time are Liz and Chris coming, then?

T Well, they should be here by now... Chris said they'd be here about half-past six... Perhaps they're on their way.

C Well, it's nearly seven... Why don't you give them a ring? Have you got their number?

T Um ... yes, somewhere... Now, where's my address book...

C Oh, it's all right, I've got it here. It's 630, double-8.

T Six-three-o-double eight, six-three-o-double-eight ... right. Now, where's the phone?

C It's just over there by the door.

T Oh, right... Now, let's see if I've got any change... Oh, no!

I've only got this. Have you got change for a pound?

C I'll have a look ... um ... No, sorry. Why don't you ask the barman?

T Yes, OK.

T Excuse me, I want to use the phone. Can you change this for me?

B Sure. What would you like? A fifty and five tens?

T Yes, that's fine, thanks.

B Right, there you go ... fifty, sixty, seventy, eighty, ninety, one pound.

T Thanks very much.

T Right, I'll give them a ring then ... um ... What was the number again? 638 something?

C No ... six-three-o double EIGHT!!!

T Right, got it. Six-three-eight ... no! six three...

Tapescript 3b

Mr G: Mr Graham   **BC 1:** Bank Clerk 1   **BC 2:** Bank Clerk 2

Mr G Excuse me, can you tell me where I can cash a traveller's cheque?

BC 1 Yes. If you just go to the 'Foreign' counter...

Mr G Oh, right ... um... There's nobody there, though.

BC 1 Well, just ring the bell, and someone'll come and attend to you.

Mr G Oh, right. OK, thanks.

BC 1 You're welcome.

BC 2 Yes, please? Can I help you?

Mr G Yes, I'd like to cash a traveller's cheque please ... in dollars...

BC 2 Right. May I see your passport, please?

Mr G Sure, here it is.

BC 2 Thank you.

Mr G What's the exchange rate today?

BC 2 It's ... um ... for dollar traveller's cheques ... 57.17 pence to the dollar.

Mr G Right... So what do I have to do here? Do I just sign...? The cheque's for $100.

BC 2 Can you just sign there, please, at the bottom.

Mr G Here?

BC 2 Yes, please.

BC 2 OK. Here's your receipt...

Mr G Thank you... Oh, what is this? You've taken off £2.

BC 2 Yes, that's the bank's commission. There's a standard charge of £2 up to £200.

Mr G Oh, I see.

BC 2 So that's twenty, forty, fifty, fifty-five pounds and ... seventeen pence.

Mr G OK. Thank you.

BC 2 Thank you. Goodbye.

Tapescript 3c

S: Suzie   **N:** Newsagent

S Um . . . do you have a magazine called *Time Out?*

N Yes, it should be over there . . . right behind you.

S Oh yes, here it is.

N So that's . . . er . . . £1.30, please.

S And can I have a book of stamps, please? . . . four first-class stamps.

N So that's one-thirty . . . two . . . two twenty-six, please.

S Oh, and a box of matches, please.

N So that's £2.26, £2.33 altogether, please.

N So that's two fifty, sixty, eighty, three, four and five. . .

S Sorry, I think you've made a mistake.

N Oh? What's that?

S I think you've given me the wrong change.

N Are you sure?

S I'm absolutely positive . . . I gave you £10, a £10 note.

N Oh, did you? I'll just go and check.

N So you did, my mistake. And five . . . is ten. Sorry about that.

S That's all right.

Tapescript 3d

1   **T: Tim   C: Claire**
    T Have you got change for a pound?
    C I'll have a look . . . um . . . No, sorry.

2   **T: Tim   B: Barman**
    T Can you change this for me?
    B Sure. What would you like? A fifty and five tens?

3   **Mr G: Mr Graham   BC 1: Bank Clerk 1**
    Mr G Can you tell me where I can cash a traveller's cheque?
    BC 1 Yes. If you just go to the 'Foreign' counter . . .

4   **Mr G: Mr Graham   BC 2: Bank Clerk 2**
    Mr G What's the exchange rate today?
    BC 2 It's . . . 57.17 pence to the dollar.

5   **S: Suzie   N: Newsagent**
    S Sorry, I think you've made a mistake.
    N Oh? What's that?

6   **S: Suzie   N: Newsagent**
    S I think you've given me the wrong change.
    N Are you sure?

Unit 4

Tapescript 4a

P: Paul   R: Restaurant

R Hello, Joanie's.

P Hello. I'd like to book a table, please, for this Friday if that's possible. . .

R Just a moment, I'd better have a look.

R . . . so that's this Friday, yes? The twenty-first?

P Yes, that's right.

R And around what time were you thinking of?

P Well, around eight o'clock. Would that be all right?

R Oh, I'm afraid we won't have anything till around nine on the twenty-first. We're rather busy. . .

P Oh, so you don't have anything at eight . . .

R No. I'm afraid we're fully booked until nine unless you want something earlier. . .

P Oh, well. Do you have anything around seven or seven-thirty?

R Yes, seven o'clock would be OK. How many people is it for?

P Well, probably four . . . there'll be four of us.

R For four people, and that's at seven o'clock. . .

P Yes, I suppose that'll be all right.

R Right. So that's a table for four people at seven on Friday the twenty-first. . .

P That's right, yes.

R Right. Could I have the name, please?

P Yes, it's Barnard, that's B-A-R-N-A-R-D.

R Barnard, right. And do you have a daytime telephone number?

P Yes, it's Oxford seven-eight-double-o-five-o.

R Sorry? Was that seven-eight-five. . . ?

P No. Seven-eight-double-o . . . five-o.

R Five . . . o. We'll look forward to seeing you on Friday, then, Mr Barnard.

P Thank you very much. See you then. 'Bye.

R 'Bye.

Tapescript 4b

RM: Restaurant manager   **W:** Waitress   **D1:** Paul (Diner 1)
D2: Diner 2   **D3:** Diner 3   **D4:** Diner 4

Dialogue 1

W Would you like a dessert?

D1 Oh, yes, I think so. . . Do you want a dessert?

D2 Oh yes!

D3 Definitely!

D1 Right! Could we have another look at the menu please?

Dialogue 2

W And what would you like to drink?

D1 Well, shall we have some wine? A bottle?

D2/3/4 Mm, yes. That'd be nice. Yes, why not?

D1 What shall we have . . . white? Red? Or rosé?

D3 Well, I'd prefer white. . .

D2 Yes, so would I.

D1 Right. White's OK for everyone, then. Could we have a bottle of house white, please.

W House white. OK.

D4 Well, I'd better not drink, 'cos I'm driving . . . could we have some mineral water as well, please? A large bottle?

Dialogue 3

RM Good evening.

D1 Hello . . . we booked a table for seven o'clock. The name's Barnard.

RM Right, yes. Here it is. How many people is it?

D1 A table for four, please.

RM Right. If you'd just like to take a seat, we'll call you over when the table's ready. Can I take your coats?

Dialogue 4

D3 Excuse me . . .

W Yes?

D3 Could we have some more coffee, please?

W Yes, of course.

Dialogue 5

D1 Does anyone want anything else? Any more coffee or anything?

D3 No, I couldn't, really! That was lovely.

D2 Perhaps we'd better ask. . .

D1 Yes. . . Excuse me! Can we have our bill, please?

Dialogue 6

W Are you ready to order?

D1 Yes, I think so. . .

W Right. Can I take the starters first? Madam?

D3 I'd like the Mediterranean prawns to start with, please.

W OK . . . and for you, madam?

D4 And for me. . .

D1 And me too. . .

W So that's three Mediterranean prawns . . . and for you, sir?

D2 Well, I'm going to have something different. . . Could you tell me what fish chowder is?

W Yes, it's a soup made with different kinds of white fish, bacon, cream, onions . . . It's really very nice. . .

D2 Oh, that sounds good. I'll have fish chowder then.

W Right, so that's three Mediterranean prawns, and one fish chowder. . . Now, what would you like for the main course?

Tapescript 4c

1 D1 I'd like to book a table, please.

2 D1 A table for four, please.

3 D2 Could you tell me what fish chowder is?

4 D2 I'll have fish chowder then.

5 D1 Could we have a bottle of house white, please?

6 W Would you like a dessert?

7 D3 Could we have some more coffee, please?

8 D1 Can we have our bill, please?

Unit 5

Tapescript 5a

A: (Shop) Assistant   **C:** Customer

a.

A Can I help you at all?

C No, I'm just looking, thanks.

A Well, if you want anything, just give me a call. . .

C Erm. . . This jumper. . . Have you got this in a large?

A No, we've only got the small and the medium, but the sizes are quite big. Try it on – the fitting room's behind here. . . There you are.

C Thanks.

A Does it fit OK?

C Yes, it fits perfectly, actually. . .

A Yes, it does. It looks really good on you. That colour suits you.

C Mmm, I don't know about the colour, myself. . . This cream's going to get very dirty. . . You couldn't pass me the greeny-coloured one, could you?

A I'm afraid I've only got that in the small. . . The brown one looks very nice on – we've got that in the medium. . .

C Mmm. . . No, I'll take this cream one, I *do* like it. . . How much was it – £11.99?

A That one's . . . £13.99 actually. . .

C Oh, well. . .! Do you take Visa?

A Sure. I'll wrap it up for you while you're getting ready. . .

b.

C Hello.

A Hello.

C Can I leave this jacket with you?

A When would you like to pick it up?

C You can't possibly do it for later this afternoon, can you?

A No, sorry. . . Tomorrow morning's the earliest we can manage. . .

C OK, fine . . . How much is it?

A It'll be six pounds, but you pay when you pick it up. Here's your ticket. Don't forget to bring it with you!

C Thanks. 'Bye. . .

c.

Cl: Clerk

C I want to send this parcel to Spain. How much will it be?

Cl Put it on the scales . . . just £2.75, please.

C Good. Will it get there before Christmas?

Cl Well, really you're too late – the last posting day for EC countries was last Saturday. But you might be lucky. . .

C OK, well, I'll try. . .

Cl £2.75 then, please. Anything else?

C Three first class stamps, please.

Cl So that's . . . £3.47. Thank you, and here are your stamps. You can just put the parcel in the post box over there. . .

d.

H: Hairdresser

H Good morning.

C Hello. . . I'd like to book a trim. . . erm, as soon as possible, please.

H We can do it now if you like. . .

C Mmm, I'm in a bit of a hurry. . .

H What about tomorrow morning . . . ten o'clock?

C No, the morning's no good for me. . . Have you got anything after about five?

H Nothing this week, I'm afraid, that's our busy time. . . No, nothing until the end of next week. . . What about next Thursday at five fifteen?

C Oh, dear. . . Well, perhaps I could stay now. . . You really can do it right now?

H Yeah, sure. . . Just a trim, you say?

C Yes, I just want half an inch off the ends.

H Do you want a wash and blow-dry or just a dry trim?

C Erm . . . yes . . . no . . . erm how much is a wash and blow-dry?

H Special offer this week . . . £14.50.

C Yes, OK, then . . . why not. . .?

H OK. If you'd like to take a seat here. . . Would you like a coffee?

e.

A: Assistant

A What can I do for you?

C These boots need re-heeling. . .

A Yeah, we can do that for you.

C Can you do them now?

A I'm a bit busy at the moment, love. Can you come back and collect them in about an hour?

C Mmmm. . . It'll have to be after lunch. . .

A No problem. Here's your ticket. You'll need that to pick them up.

C Thanks then. 'Bye. . .

Tapescript 5b

A Can I help you at all?

C No, I'm just looking, thanks.

A Well, if you want anything, just give me a call. . .

C Erm. . . This jumper. . . Have you got this in a large?

A No, we've only got the small and the medium, but the sizes are quite big. Try it on – the fitting room's behind here. . . There you are.

C Thanks.

A Does it fit OK?

C Yes, it fits perfectly, actually. . .

A Yes, it does. It looks really good on you. That colour suits you.

C Mmm, I don't know about the colour, myself. . . This cream's going to get very dirty. . .

Unit 6

Tapescript 6a

1

J: Jayne **M:** (Recorded) Message

J Hello. Could you tell me the train times to – oh!

M Welcome to British Rail's talking timetable service, giving a summary of principal Monday to Friday train services leaving London Waterloo for Southampton and Bournemouth until 12th May, except Bank and Public Holidays.

Fast services leave London Waterloo at 08.15, 09.32, and 32 minutes past each hour until 16.32. Then 17.15, 18.32, and 19.32. Journey time to Southampton is 69 minutes, and to Bournemouth 99 minutes. Refreshments are available on all services. . .

2

T: Telephonist **J:** Jayne **M:** Man

T Good afternoon, Magenta Advertising Services.

J Hello. Can I have extension 248, please?

T It's ringing for you.

M Hello, Marketing.

J Hello. Can I speak to Julie Mitchell, please?

M Um . . . Could you hold on a moment, please. I'll just check where she is. . . Hello? Sorry, she's in a meeting at the moment. . . I'm afraid she'll be busy for another hour or so. . . Can I take a message?

J Yes, please, if you would. . . Could you tell her that Jayne White phoned?

M Jayne. . . White. . . OK.

J And could you ask her to ring me at home this afternoon, before four if she can? It's nothing urgent. It's just about next week.

M Right... Does she have the number?

J I think so, but just in case, it's... Have you got a pen?

M Yeah...

J So, it's six-nine-two...

M Six-nine-two, yeah?

J Four-double five-o.

M Right... Is that a London number?

J Yeah, it's o-eight-one...

M OK, I'll give her the message.

J OK. Thanks very much indeed. 'Bye.

M 'Bye.

3

J: Jayne   **M:** (Recorded) Message

J Right, now for that wretched plumber... Hello? Is that JDT Plu- Oh, no!

M Hello, this is JDT Plumbing and Heating Services Ltd. I'm afraid there's no one in our office to take your call at the moment, but if you leave your name and number we'll get back to you as soon as we can. Please speak after the tone. Thank you.

J Yes. This is Jayne White. That's W-H-I-T-E... You promised to send me a plumber this *morning*, to 15 Aberdeen Place, W10 ... and it's now nearly three o'clock, and no one's here yet. Could you *please* tell me if I can expect someone this afternoon... If not, I'll have to try another plumber. The number is 692 4550. Thank you.

4

J: Jayne   **P:** Peter (her young brother)

P 764 9400.

J Oh, hi, Peter. It's me... How's my little brother?

P Less of the little!

J I see. Well, is Mum there?

P No, she's just gone out to the supermarket... She'll be back in a minute.

J Well, you know I said I'd be coming down from London to see you all this afternoon...

P Oh, really?

J Yes, I did tell you, actually... Well, anyway, I'm going to be a bit later than I thought... I've got to wait for the plumber... I'm going to try and get the 16.32, so I should be there about eight, a bit before... OK? Can you tell Mum?

P OK. Shall I ask Dad to come and pick you up from the station?

J No, it's all right. I'll get a taxi.

P OK. I'll see you a bit later, then.

J OK. 'Bye.

P 'Bye.

Tapescript 6b

a. Hello. Could you tell me the train times to ...

b. Hello. Can I have extension 248, please?

c. Hello. Marketing.
Hello. Can I speak to Julie Mitchell, please?

d. Um ... Could you hold on a moment, please. I'll just check...

e. She'll be busy for another hour or so... Can I take a message?

f. Could you tell her that Jayne White phoned? Jayne ... White ... OK?

g. And could you ask her to ring me at home this afternoon, before four if she can?

h. Hello? Is that JDT Plu-

i. Yes. This is Jayne White. That's W-H-I-T-E...

j. Oh, hi, Peter. It's me ...

k. Is Mum there?

Unit 7

Tapescript 7a

T: Traveller   **O:** Information official

O Can I help you?

T Yes, please. Is there somewhere here where I can hire a car?

O Yes... You go straight on past these shops here, on the right...

T Uh-huh...

O ... and you turn right just before the toilets... The car hire office is on your left, in a corner... It's next to the Bureau de Change.

T Thank you very much.

O Thank you.

Tapescript 7b

T1: Tourist 1   **T2:** Tourist 2   **O:** Tourist Information
official

T1 Hello. We're looking for a cheap place to stay – something fairly central.

O Right... How many people is it for?

T1 Just the two of us.

O Mm... Let's have a look... Things are rather busy at the moment, I'm afraid... There aren't many vacancies in the hotels at the moment – that we know of ... just a moment...
... Ah! There's a double room still vacant at the Dolphin Hotel... That's a small hotel. Is that any good?

T2 Whereabouts is it?

O It's about a mile and a half outside the centre of town, but there's a very good bus service...

T1 Mm... We were hoping for something a little more central, but if that's all there is... How do we get there?

O I'll show you on this map. Right. You take bus number 17 from just outside this office, and ask the driver to tell you when you get to the stop just *before* St. Gilbert's hospital. Anyway, you'll know you're there because you go past a big cemetery on your left just before you have to get off.

T2 So, the stop just *before* the hospital.

O That's right, and then you're here... If you just look at the map...

T1 Yeah.

O So when you get off, you cross the road and go up Cavendish Avenue, here. Then you walk along there for about 200 metres, past this church here on the left. The next road is Lavender Drive, and the Dolphin's just there, on the right-hand corner of Lavender Drive and Cavendish Avenue... It's only a few minutes from the bus stop. It'll take you about twenty minutes altogether.

T2 Right. Thanks a lot. Can we take the map?

O Yes, of course.

T1 Thanks very much ... cheers!

Tapescript 7c

W: a woman **M:** a man

W Hello. I've arranged to meet one of the teachers here. Can you tell me where the staff room is?

M Yes, you go through this set of doors here. Go past the main staircase, straight on through the next set of doors, past another little staircase, and just follow the corridor round as far as you can go, and the staff room's right at the end, next to the ladies' toilets.

W Thank you very much indeed.

Tapescript 7d

a. ... Is there somewhere here where I can hire a car?

b. ... You go straight on past these shops...

c. ... It's next to the Bureau de Change.

d. ... How do we get there?

e. ... Then you walk along there for about 200 metres.

f. ... the Dolphin's just there, on the right hand corner of Lavender Drive and Cavendish Avenue...

g. ... Can you tell me where the staff room is?

h. Yes, you go through this set of doors here...

i. ... Go past the main staircase...

Unit 8

Tapescript 8a

P: Philip **R:** Receptionist

R Good morning, Queen's Hotel...

P Hello. I'd like to make a reservation, please.

R Certainly, sir. Can I have the name, please?

P Yes. The name's Beaumont... That's B-E-A-U-M-O-N-T.

R Right. So it's Mr Beaumont...

P Well, actually, it's for my mother. That's *Mrs* Beaumont, Mrs Joan Beaumont, J-O-A-N.

R Mrs Joan Beaumont. Fine. When would you like the reservation for?

P It's for three nights, from the 26th to the 28th.

R Right. So that's three nights from the 26th to the 28th of October.

P That's right.

R Is that a single or a double room?

P A single, please, on the ground floor if that's possible.

R I'll just check if that's available.

I'm afraid we only have twin rooms available on the ground floor. Would that be OK?

P Erm... Yes, I'm sure that would be fine. Could you tell me the price, please?

R Certainly. That's £65 per night... That's including breakfast.

P I see, OK...

R Could I have the address and phone number, please?

P What, *my* address?

R Well, it's for your mother, isn't it? So perhaps you could give me her address...

P Yes, certainly. It's 46 ... Nunthorpe Road, that's N-U-N-T-H-O-R-P-E Road...

R Nunthorpe, yes...

P York.

R OK. And the telephone number?

P ... Is 0904 25567.

R 0-9-0-4–2-5-5-6-7.

P Right.

R Right. So that's a twin room on the ground floor for Mrs J Beaumont from the 26th to the 28th of October.

P That's right, yes.

R OK then, Mr Beaumont. Thank you very much for calling.

P Thank you. Goodbye.

R Goodbye.

Tapescript 8b

B: Mrs Beaumont   **R:** Receptionist

B Good morning. I've got a reservation. My name's Beaumont. Mrs Joan Beaumont.

R Right. I'll just check, Mrs. Beaumont...

R Yes, Mrs. Beaumont. We have your reservation here on the computer. It's a twin room...

B Yes, that's right.

R ... with shower ...

B With shower? Oh no, that's not right. I distinctly told my son to ask for a *twin* room with a *bath*... I must have a bath, you see, because of my bad back ... Oh, really!

R Not to worry, Mrs Beaumont, we can easily transfer your reservation to a room with bath...

B Really!

R Right. We can give you room 452. That's a twin room with bath...

B Room 452?

R Yes, would that be OK?

B Well, I suppose...

R Right... Could you take this lady's bags up to Room 452?

B Just a moment ... Room 452... Which floor is that on?

R It's on the fourth floor.

B Oh, but I can't possibly have a room on the fourth floor... It's my back, you see. I can't possibly manage all those stairs...

R Well, we *do* have a *lift*, Mrs Beaumont...

B Yes, but all the same ... I definitely asked my son to ask for a room on the *ground* floor...

R Well, I'm afraid all the rooms on the ground floor are with shower only.

B Oh, how annoying!

R I'm sure you'll find the lift very convenient ... and there aren't any stairs for you to climb.

B Oh, well ... I suppose so...

R I'm sure it'll be fine, Mrs Beaumont... And you'll be staying for three nights, is that right?

B *Three* nights? No, no, it's *four* nights. I'm staying till Tuesday morning... Oh, it's that son of mine again! ...

R Well, Mrs Beaumont, we can easily change that. I'll just change your reservation on the computer...

B It's all my son's fault, I'm sure... When I see him, I'll...

R Not to worry, Mrs Beaumont. Well, if you wouldn't mind filling in this form...

Tapescript 8c

a. **R** Good morning, Queen's Hotel...

   P Hello. I'd like to make a reservation, please.

b. **P** It's for three nights, from the 26th to the 28th.

c. **P** Could you tell me the price, please?

d. **R** Can I have the name, please?

   P Yes. The name's Beaumont.

e. **R** When would you like the reservation for?

f. **R** Is that a single or a double room?

Unit 9

Tapescript 9a

A: Annie   **W:** Woman

1

W Hello. Lucinda Gray speaking.

A Er... Hello ... erm, I'm phoning about the room you've advertised...

W Oh, yes. Actually it's my brother you should speak to. It's his flat, and I'm afraid he's not here at the moment...

A Oh, I see...

W Perhaps you could phone back later this evening? He should be home after 9.00.

A Yes, right, I will... Who should I ask for?

W Richard Gray.

A OK. Thank you very much then... Goodbye.

W Goodbye. Thank you for calling.

2

A: Annie   **M:** Man

M Hello. 579 8118.

A Hello. I'm phoning about the room you advertised...

M Oh, I'm sorry, it's gone. We found someone at the weekend.

A Oh, right... Thank you very much then...

M Yes, thanks for calling. 'Bye.

A 'Bye.

3

A: Annie   **M:** Man

M Hello.

A Hello. Could I speak to Andrew please?

M Yes, that's me.

A Oh, right... I'm phoning about the room you advertised. Is it still available?

M Yes, sure...

A Er... Can you tell me something about the room and the house and everything?

M Well... What can I tell you...? You know the price from the advert... It's a really nice room – very big and sunny and ... well ... It's a nice house too... There are two of us

go to bed for a couple of days and take paracetamol for the headache.

Dan But you can't give me any medicine. . .

Doc Not for the virus, as I said. But I think you also have an ear infection, and I'm going to give you some antibiotics for that . . . to help the earache. I'll just give you a prescription.

Dan Right.

Doc So . . . you take one of these tablets four times a day . . . OK?

Dan Yes.

Doc And it's very important that you finish the prescription – that you take *all* the tablets.

Dan So how many days will that be?

Doc Er . . . five days. . . That's four tablets a day for five days. OK?

Dan Yes, sure. Where do I go to get the prescription?

Doc There's a chemist's just near here. . . You go out, turn left . . . and it's about fifty yards up the road, on your left.

Dan Thank you. . . Oh, I'm not British, so will I have to pay anything?

Doc No, just the normal prescription charge. . .

Dan OK. Thank you very much. . . Goodbye.

Doc 'Bye.

Unit 12

Tapescript 12a

R: Rachel   **M:** Max

R Here's your coffee, Max.

M Thanks.

R So how are things? You've finished your exams already, haven't you?

M Yeah, we finished them yesterday. . . Now I'm looking for a job!

R Seriously?

M Yes, seriously. I have to, Rachel. I haven't got any money, and I really don't want to go home to my family in Rotterdam yet. . .

R And are you allowed to work in Britain? I mean don't you need a work permit or anything?

M No, no. Not if you're an EC citizen. You can work just the same as an English person. There's no problem at all. . .

R That's good. . . I didn't know that. . . So what kind of thing are you looking for?

M Just something in a bar or a restaurant. It doesn't really matter. . . Maybe in a shop. . . The problem is I don't really know *how* to look for a job in this country. . . What do people usually do?

R Well you could go to the Job Centre, or look in the newspaper. . . Have you tried looking in the *Evening Telegraph?*

M I looked yesterday, but there weren't any job adverts. . .

R Well, there might be some today. . . Actually I think I've got a *Telegraph* in my bag. . . Yeah, here it is. Shall we have a look now?

M Why not? I tell you what – you start looking and I'll get us some biscuits, OK?

R Great. . .

Tapescript 12b

M: Max   **R:** Rachel

M Anything interesting?

R One or two things. . . What about this. . . ? 'Sandwich makers required. Sunday 7 a.m. to 11 a.m., Monday to Thursday 6 a.m. to 10 a.m. Wages £2.50 per hour.'

M Mmm, I want something more full-time. . . It's not many hours . . . and starting work at 6 a.m.! No, I don't think that's for me. . .

R Well how about this then? 'Spanish restaurant requires chef and assistant bar staff, couple considered. . .'

M Yes, I could try that, couldn't I? I mean, I'm not Spanish, but. . .

R Now what about this? 'Reception/Bar vacancies in busy central Night Club. Good rates of pay, taxi home, meal provided. . . Hours 8.30 p.m. to 2.30 a.m. . . . .'

M That sounds good – yes!

R Ah, now this is a good one for you, Max. . . 'Staff required to sell hot dogs, ice-cream, and hamburgers. . .'

M I am *not* selling hot dogs! You know I hate the smell of onions! No, the night club sounds the best, definitely. . .

R Well, phone them!

M What, now. . . ?

R Yes, go on!

Tapescript 12c

W: Woman   **M:** Max

W Hello?

M I'm phoning about your advertisement for reception and bar staff in the *Evening Telegraph.*

W Yes.

M Can you tell me something about the bar job?

W I think most of the details are in the advert. It's 8.30 to 2.30. There's a meal provided and a taxi home if you need one. The hourly rate is £3.50 plus bonus, and bar staff wear a uniform.

M £3.50 you said?

W That's right.

M What do I do if I want to apply?

W Come in and speak to Jane... I suppose it's too late for you to come in this afternoon?

M Well ... yes...

W The next time she's here is Wednesday evening, so come in about 9.00.

M Wednesday evening about 9.00... Whereabouts are you?

W 112 Brighton Road... You know where that is, don't you?

M 112 Brighton Road... Yes, I know that...

W And remember to ask for Jane...

M Yes, I will. OK, then. Thank you... Goodbye.

W Goodbye.

Tapescript 12d

W: Woman   **M:** Max

W Hello?

M I'm *phoning about* your advertisement for reception and bar staff in the *Evening Telegraph.*

W Yes.

M Can you *tell me something about* the bar job?

W I think most of the details are *in the advert.* It's 8.30 to 2.30. There's a meal provided and a *taxi home* if you need one. The *hourly rate* is £3.50 *plus bonus,* and bar staff *wear a uniform.*

M What do I do if I want *to apply?*

Unit 13

Tapescript 13

B: Mrs Bolton   **E:** Elena

1

B Right. Elena...

E Um ... it's Elena, Mrs Bolton ... Elena.

B Oh, I'm so sorry dear ... Elena... Well, I've shown you how the dishwasher works... Now, what else do you need to know? Ah yes, you'll definitely be using this... The children get their things so dirty...

E Right... How does it work exactly?

B It's really very simple... I'll show you. It's plugged in at the wall here... So you put the clothes in here... Then the powder... I use about half a cupful for a normal wash... That goes in this drawer here...

E I see.

B ... And you turn this dial to the programme you want... I usually use number one... And the rest is automatic, really...

E Right. That seems very easy. What's this dial for?

B Ah, that's for the drier... I don't usually use that... You see it uses such a lot of electricity, Elena, and ...

E It's Elena, Mrs Bolton, Elena.

B Oh, I'm so sorry, dear... Elena... Well now, I wonder what else you need to know about...

2

M: Man   **W:** Woman

M Right... So it's... Programme Starts ... 3 o'clock...

W Are you OK with that?

M Yes, thank you, darling. I can manage.

W Well, all right. It's just that last time you tried to record something...

M Yes, I know, I know. But I understand it now, thank you very much. Now, it's 3 o'clock ... and it's Channel ... oh! It's flashing on and off! Why's it doing that?

W I don't know... What've you done to it? OK. Now which button did you press?

M This one... Timer something...

W OK. Well you just press it again ... that's it... Programme Ends ... what time does this football match finish, then?

M Er ... about about 5 o'clock, I think.

W Right, so Programme Ends ... 5 o'clock ... Channel Four is it?

M No, it's Channel Three...

W Channel Three... There, you see? Easy!

M Hmmm... Anyway, what if I want to record another programme after that one?

W Well, you just press this button here and you do the same thing again... Look, why don't you just look in the instruction book? It's perfectly simple... Just read what it says instead of asking me all these stupid questions ...

3

GD: Grandad   **GS:** Grandson

GD Oh, that looks complicated... Are you sure you really understand all that?

GS Yes, Grandad. It's easy...

GD Easy for you, maybe... There was nothing like this when I was your age...

GS There's nothing to it, really! Look, I'll show you. You just put the disk in here ... this way ... till it clicks... You switch on...

GD Nothing's happening! What's wrong with it?

GS Nothing. You just have to wait for a minute ... and ... DA! DA! You've got the menu!

GD The *what?!*

GS The menu . . . OK, so say I want to open this file here. . . I just move the arrows . . . and press ENTER. . .

GD Enter? What's 'enter'?

GS And you get the file on the screen there. . . You see?

GD Hmm. . . Very nice. Tell me something, what happens if I press this button here?

GS You lose the file, Grandad.

GD Oh, dear. Why isn't there anything on the screen?

Unit 14

Tapescript 14

C: Claudia **O:** Mrs Owen **J:** Jenny **R:** Robbie

C It's really kind of you to bring me to the station, Mrs Owen. It really is!

O You're welcome, dear. It's the least I could do. Now, which platform do you want? Let's see, does that say platform 16 for London King's Cross? My eyes aren't very good. . .

C No, it's 15. It leaves at 12.46.

O So we've got about twenty minutes. Do you want to go and have a coffee?

C Well, actually a couple of friends said they'd come and say goodbye and I said I'd meet them here. . . Oh, look! That's Jenny now – JENNY!!!

J Claudia, hi! I thought perhaps you'd already gone. . .

C This is Jenny, Mrs Owen. . . This is Mrs Owen, my landlady.

O How do you do, dear?

J How do you do, Mrs Owen. Claudia, I'm really sorry, but I can only stay a couple of minutes. I've got to get back to work. . .

C Jenny works in the same sandwich shop that I was working in. That's how we met.

O Oh, you work in the sandwich shop too, do you? It's hard work, from what Claudia tells me.

J It certainly *is*, but the people are really, really nice. So it's not so bad. . . Claudia, is that Robbie over there?

C Oh, yes, so it is. . .

O And who's Robbie, Claudia? Is this the latest boyfriend? I've never known a girl with so many boyfriends!

J This one's serious, Mrs Owen. He says he's going to leave his job in Edinburgh after the summer, and go and live in Milan, to be with Claudia. Isn't that right, Claudia?

C We'll see. . . ROBBIE!!! We're here!

R Hi. I'm really sorry I'm late. I had problems parking the car. . . Hi, there, Jenny.

J Hi.

C Robbie, this is Mrs Owen, my landlady, who's very kindly given me a lift to the station.

R Nice to meet you Mrs Owen. Claudia's told me a lot about you.

O How do you do, Robbie. Very pleased to meet you.

J I'm really sorry, Claudia, I'll have to get back to work. . . I just wanted to say have a good journey and do write. We'll all miss you!

C I'll miss all of you too. Send my love to everyone at work.

J I will.

C And remember, you're always welcome in Milan, if you ever want to come to Italy. . .

J Well, I really hope I'll be able to come before I go back to New Zealand. . .

O Actually, I think I'd better get back to the car, too. I'll leave you two young people to say goodbye on your own. . .

C Oh, no. Don't be silly, Mrs Owen. . .

O No, really. I'd better be off. Now, take care of yourself, my dear, and do give my regards to your mother. . .

C Yes, I will. And you look after yourself too. . . And again, thank you very, very much for everything. I've had a wonderful time. . .

O It's been a pleasure, dear. . . And good luck with your exams in October. . .

J Oh, yes, your exams. . . Good luck. Don't work too hard!

C Don't worry. . .

O 'Bye then, dear.

C 'Bye, and thanks for everything. . .

J 'Bye! Keep in touch!

C I will . . . 'Bye. . .

J See you, Robbie. . .

R Yeah, see you around. . . Let's go for a quick coffee, Claudia, so that we can say goodbye properly.

C OK then. . .

Card 2

1 You are at the airport information desk (map 1) and want to know where there's a flower shop in the airport.
2 You are at the bus stop opposite the hospital (map 2) and want to know where the Park Gates Hotel is.
3 You are at the reception desk in the school and want to know where the computer centre is.

Answers to A's questions
– the telephones are at B on map 1.
– the George Hotel is D on map 2 (you are at the bus stop opposite the hospital).
– the Director's office is D on map 3.

Answer key

Unit 1 Getting around

Before you listen 1

Train	Underground	Aeroplane	Bus	Taxi
a fare	a fare	a fare	a fare	a fare
a departure board	the tube	a departure board	a conductor	to drop someone off
a platform	a platform	passengers	a double-decker	passengers
passengers	to change lines	a single ticket	passengers	
a single ticket	passengers	a return ticket		
a return ticket	a single ticket			
	a return ticket			

Listening for information

1   a. To visit his girlfriend in Italy.   c. Because he is working until six o'clock.
    b. On Friday the 21st, at 8.30.   d. How to get to his office, from Heathrow.

2   1 Tube   2 Bus   3 Train   4 Taxi

3
From Heathrow, Underground to <u>Green Park</u> station (Piccadilly Line takes about <u>45</u> minutes).
Bus number <u>38</u> or <u>25</u> to Victoria (bus stop <u>opposite</u> tube station).
From Victoria, fast train to Brighton at <u>6</u> minutes past the hour (takes <u>less than an hour</u>).
(Other trains take <u>an hour and a quarter.</u>)

David's office
Davis International, <u>55 Seaview</u> Road.

Listening for language

1   1 bus (On trains and tubes you pay before   5 taxi
        you get on.)   6 train
    2 train   7 taxi
    3 tube (This is an announcement that is only   8 bus
        used on the Underground.)   9 bus/train/tube
    4 train   10 bus (With tubes and trains you ask for a
                                                        single or a *return*.)

2/3 1 Any   3 doors ... passengers   5 Where   7 keep   9 free
     2 late departure   4 Platform ... calling   6 right   8 catch 10 One

Unit 2

Listening for information

Going out

1
a. on Sunday
b. go to the theatre/see a musical/see *Miss Saigon*
c. It will probably be difficult to get tickets.
d. the number of a ticket agency (Ticketmaster)
e. They decide that Cindy will telephone tomorrow to try to get tickets for *Miss Saigon*. If she can't, she'll try to get tickets for another musical (*Starlight Express*).

2
d. are the right tickets

Listening for language

1
The phrases that are used in Cindy and Aileen's conversation are:

1 b. 2 a. 3 a. 4 b. 5 b. 6 a.

Unit 3

Before you listen

Dealing with money

4
cash a cheque = person b.
has the wrong change = person c.
needs some change = person a.
pay commission = person b.
given a receipt = person b.

Listening for information

T.3a

1
a. 63088   b. £1 coin   c. from the barman   d. 50p piece and 5 × 10p pieces

T.3b

2
Currency = dollars
Exchange Rate = 57.17p (to the dollar)
Amount = $100
Commission = £2
Net Total = £55.17

T.3c

3
a. Picture 2   b. £2.33   c. £10   d. £2.67   e. The newsagent gives her the wrong change.

Listening for language

1
1 Have you got *change for a pound?*
2 Can you change *this for me?*
3 Can you tell me where *I can cash a traveller's cheque?*
4 What's the *exchange rate today?*
5 Sorry, I think you've *made a mistake.*
6 I think you've given me *the wrong change.*

Speaking

1
Dialogue a. in a school   Dialogue b. in a bank/Bureau de Change   Dialogue c. in a taxi

---

Unit 4

Before you listen

Eating out

3
to book a table	R	a menu	R
a dessert	R/H	mineral water	R/H
fully booked	R	to order	R
house wine	R	to pay the bill	R
a main course	R/H	a starter	R/H

Listening for information

1
Table booking
Date Friday, 21st October
Time 7.00 p.m.
Number of people Four
Name (Mr) Barnard
Tel No Oxford 780050

2	Arriving at the restaurant	3	Ordering more wine	–
	Ordering starters	6	Deciding about dessert	1
	Ordering a main course	–	Asking for more coffee	· 4
	Ordering something to drink	2	Asking for the bill	5

Listening for language   **1/2**   The correct sentences are:

1 b. 2 a. 3 b. 4 b. 5 b. 6 b. 7 a. 8 a.

Unit 5   Shopping

Before you listen   **2**

Hairdresser's	Clothes shop	Post office	Heel bar	Dry cleaner's
a trim	a fitting room	a parcel	re-heeling	
a wash and blow dry	a jumper			
	the medium size			
	to fit someone			
	to suit someone			

Listening for information   **1/2**

1 Shop	2 What the customer wants/buys	3 Money to pay	4 Minor problems
a. clothes shop	(cream medium-sized) jumper	£13.99	They haven't got the cream jumper in a large.
b. dry cleaner's	to have his jacket cleaned	£6 (not now, tomorrow)	They can't clean it until tomorrow morning.
c. post office	– to send a parcel to Spain – three first class stamps	£3.47	The last posting date for Christmas was last Saturday for EC countries.
d. hairdresser's	a trim and a wash and blow dry	£14.50	There are no appointments after 5.00 until Thursday next week.
e. heel bar	to have her boots re-heeled	–	The assistant can't re-heel them right now.

Listening for language	1	The correct order is

1 e.   2 d.   3 h.   4 a.   5 f.   6 c.   7 b.   8 g.   9 j.   10 i.

Unit 6

On the phone

Listening for information

1
- a. every hour
- b. just over an hour
- c. Julie should ring her back.
- d. 692 4550

2
- a. the answering machine
- b. this morning
- c. her young brother
- d. (just before) eight o'clock this evening

Listening for language

1
- a. Hello. *Could* you *tell* me the train times to...
- b. Hello. Can I *have* extension 248, please?
- c. Hello. Marketing.
    Hello. *Can* I speak *to* Julie Mitchell, please?
- d. Um ... Could you *hold on* a moment, please. I'll just check ...
- e. She'll be busy for another hour or so ... Can I *take* a *message*?
- f. *Could* you *tell* her that Jayne White *phoned*?
    Jayne ... White ... OK?
- g. And could you *ask* her to *ring* me at home this afternoon, before four if she can?
- h. *Hello*? Is *that* JDT Plu-
- i. Yes. *This* is Jayne White. That's W-H-I-T-E...
- j. Oh, hi, Peter. *It's me*...
- k. Is Mum *there*?

2   1 h.   2 f./g.   3 a.   4 e.   5 c.   6 k.   7 i./j. (i. is more formal)   8 b.   9 d.   10 f./i.

Unit 7

Asking the way

Before you listen

2   The places on the chart could be in:

a library	2, 3	a canteen	3
a car hire office	1, 2	a cemetery	2
a staff room	3	a corridor	1, 3
a staircase	1, 3	a hospital	2
a bus stop	1, 2	a church	2
a Bureau de Change	1, 2	an arrivals lounge	1

3   The places appear on the following maps:

a library	3	a canteen	3
a car hire office	1	a cemetery	2
a staff room	3	a corridor	3
a staircase	3	a hospital	2
a bus stop	2	a church	2
a Bureau de Change	1	an arrivals lounge	1

| **Listening for information** | **1** | (Best summary) |

|T.7a| (Airport) b. |T.7b| (Tourist information) a. |T.7c| (Language school) c.

2 The speakers are talking about:

|T.7a| D |T.7b| B |T.7c| A

Listening for language   **1/2**   a. I can   b. on   c. next to   d. get   e. along   f. on   g. tell   h. through   i. Go past

---

Unit 8

Booking in to a hotel

Before you listen   **1**

ground floor = floor of a building level with the street outside
first floor = immediately above the ground floor

a lift
     =   There is no difference in meaning, although lift is more commonly used in
an elevator   British English, and elevator in US English.

a bath   =    a shower =

a single room = a hotel room with one bed, for one person.
a twin room = a hotel room with two beds, for two people.

Listening for information   **1**

Philip's mother is planning to come and visit her son in Cambridge.
She wants her son to book a hotel room for her.

2

Name MR (MRS) MS MISS	Initials	Type of room	Price	Date of arrival	Date of departure	Address Tel. home / work
BEAUMONT	J	TWIN	£65	26ᵗʰ OCT	28ᵗʰ OCT	46 Nunthorpe Road York (0904) 25567

3   **Problem 1** The room has a shower instead of a bath.
Solution 1 The receptionist transfers her booking to a room with bath.
Problem 2 The new room is on the fourth floor. Mrs Beaumont cannot manage the stairs.
Solution 2 The receptionist tells her she can use the lift.
Problem 3 Mrs Beaumont has been booked in for three nights instead of four.
Solution 3 The receptionist changes her booking to four nights.

Listening for language   **1/2**   The correct order for the sentences is:

a. I'd like to make a reservation, please.
b. It's for three nights, from the 26th to the 28th.
c. Could you tell me the price, please?
d. Can I have the name, please?
e. When would you like the reservation for?
f. Is that a single or a double room?

Unit 9

Listening for information

Looking for somewhere to live

3
a. 3 and 4
b. She arranges to see 3 at 7.00 tomorrow night.
   She arranges to see 4 at 6.30 on Wednesday evening.
c. The owner of the flat in 1 is not there, so she has to ring back later. Room 2 is no longer available. They found someone to rent it at the weekend.

4

	Room itself	Rent/bills	Transport / local area	Other people living there	Address
Barnes	– nice – very large – sunny	╳	– no underground – lots of buses – near B.R. – lots of shops, – pubs, restaurants	– Andrew – Katie (a nurse)	15 Grove Road
Ealing	– large – not much furniture – nice	£240 a month – plus phone bill	╳	– Linda – Sophie (away a lot)	22 Mount Park Road

Listening for language

1/2 The correct order is:

1 d. 2 h. 3 a. 4 f. 5 k. 6 e. 7 b. 8 c. 9 i. 10 j. 11 g.

Unit 10

Listening for information

Meeting new people

1 They mention: the dog   food   the Hunts' house and garden   tea   Chris and Fran's journey to Leeds   Fran's studies

2
a. To take off his glasses.
b. Friendly and gentle.
c. 1.00 (or just after)
d. She says that the house and garden are lovely, and that the big trees in the garden are beautiful.
e. Spanish and Russian.
f. She would like to become an interpreter.
g. She is on a diet.
h. A sandwich.

Listening for language

1/2
b. Chris to Mrs Hunt
c. Chris to Mrs Hunt
d. Chris to Fran
e. Fran to Mrs Hunt/Mrs Hunt to Fran/Fran to Mr Hunt
f. Mrs Hunt to Fran
g. Mrs Hunt to Fran
h. Mrs Hunt to Fran
i. Mr Hunt to Fran
j. Mrs Hunt to Fran
k. Mrs Hunt to Chris and Fran
l. Mrs Hunt to Chris and Fran

3 b. and d. are more *informal.*   e. and i. are more *formal.*

4 The answer is also *How do you do. (How do you do.* is not a question asking for information, so it has no question mark.)

Unit 11

Before you listen

1

At the doctor's

Medical problems		What you do when you're ill	
have an ear infection	have a sore throat	take your temperature	take antibiotics
have a headache	aches and pains	go to the surgery	pay a prescription charge
have earache	a virus	get a prescription	go to the chemist's

2 The suggested order is:

1 Daniel woke up with a sore throat and earache.
2 He went to the doctor's surgery.
3 Daniel spoke to the receptionist.
4 Daniel filled in a form.
5 He saw the doctor.
6 Daniel told the doctor what was wrong.
7 The doctor told him he had an ear infection.
8 The doctor wrote a prescription.
9 Daniel paid a prescription charge at the chemist's.
10 Daniel took the paracetamol and antibiotics.
11 He felt better.

Listening for information

1/2 a. True b. True c. False (three weeks) d. True e. False (The doctor can see him this morning.) f. True

3 The correct order for the pictures is: 1 c. 2 d. 3 a. 4 e. 5 g. 6 h. 7 b. 8 f.

Listening for language

1/2 Sentences a., d., e., h., i., j., l., and o. would be said by the patient.
Sentences b., c., f., g., k., m., n., and p. would be said by the doctor.
Daniel actually said sentences a., e., i., and j.
The doctor actually said sentences b., m., n., and p.

Unit 12

Before you listen

2

Looking for a job

full-time work – working for all of each working week (usually about 40 hours)
part-time work – working for just part of each normal working week or day
job advertisement/advert – newspaper announcement about a vacant job
wage(s) – money paid (usually at the end of a week) for doing a job
hourly rate – money paid for each hour worked
work permit – official paper saying that you can work in a foreign country
bonus – extra money that you get as well as your usual pay
EC citizen – a citizen of a European Community country

Listening for information

1 Max mentions:
exams – He says he has just finished his exams.
his money problems – He says he must find a job.
the type of job he would like – He says he would like to work in a restaurant, bar, or shop.
work permit – He says he does not need one because he is from an EC country.
how to look for a job – He doesn't know how to do this in Britain, and asks Rachel's advice.

2 a. They discuss a., c., d., and e. b. He is interested in d. and e.
c. He is not interested in a. because it is not many hours and because he would have to start work very early. He is not interested in c. because he hates the smell of onions.

3 He writes note b.

Listening for language

1/2 Answers in tapescript 12d in italics.

Unit 13

Using machines

Before you listen   **2**

channel:	TV
dial:	radio/washing machine
disk:	computer
drawer:	washing machine/dishwasher
file:	computer
menu:	computer
to plug in:	coffee machine/video recorder/dishwasher/washing machine/radio/computer/TV
to press a button:	all of the machines in the picture
to record:	Walkman/video recorder
screen:	TV/computer
to switch on/off:	all of the machines

Listening for information   **1**

Relationship between speakers	Machine being discussed
1 au pair (maid) and employer	1 washing machine
2 husband and wife/boyfriend and girlfriend/friends	2 video recorder
3 grandfather and grandson	3 computer

T.13   **2**

1a. half a cupful   b. number one   c. Because it uses a lot of electricity.
2a. Yes   b. a football match   c. It starts at 3.00 and finishes at 5.00.
3a. He thinks they are complicated.   b. He thinks they are easy.   c. He loses the file.

Listening for language   **1/2**

1 c.   2 e.   3 f.   4 d.   5 a.   6 b.

Unit 14

Saying goodbye

Listening for information   **1/2**

1 Claudia works in a *sandwich shop*, not a pub.
2 Claudia is from *Milan*, not Rome.
3 Jenny is Claudia's *friend from work*, not her room-mate.
4 Jenny is from *New Zealand*, not Australia.
5 Robbie *is not going to Italy now*. He wants to move there after the summer.

Listening for language   **1/2**

a. Claudia   b. Mrs Owen   c. Robbie   d. Jenny   e. Claudia   f. Mrs Owen   g. Claudia h. Jenny

3   1a. Thank you   b. Hello   c. Hello   d. Goodbye   e. Goodbye   f. Goodbye
g. Thank you   h. Goodbye

2 See the tapescript on page 72 for suitable answers.

3 b. (*How do you do.*) and f. (*Do give my regards to your mother.*) are more formal. This is because Mrs Owen is an older person.